How to Write Lots, and Get Sh*t Done: the Art of Not Being a Flake

Jess Mountifield

How to Write Lots, and Get Sh*t Done: the Art of Not Being a Flake

ISBN-13: 9798612841159

TO ELLA

Without you there would be no books at all

Contents

INTRODUCTION

It's New Year's Day 2020. This is one of those magical times of the year when people are thinking about what they want to achieve, how they want to achieve it, and if it's truly even possible.

Ten years ago and one day I finished my very first novel. Since then I've written over two millions words of fiction, had two tiny humans and coached tens of writers along the path to being a productive author themselves. I've gone from writing an average of 300 words per hour to 2000, and I've gone from barely writing one book a year to being able to write about 20.

For a long time I had a very lax approach to my career. I wrote when I felt like it, played games when I didn't, and generally didn't make an awful lot of money.

And then one day I gave birth. Thankfully I'd known it was coming. But I hadn't been prepared. Not truly.

I'm not sure anything can prepare a person for how much a baby changes things, but I hadn't understood how much I needed to create, how much writing felt like breathing, until it was too late.

The next year of my life was chaos as I tried to work out a strategy to fit my writing back in and produce consistent work. In that time my career died, my book ranks declined and I was left feeling very bitter.

But I didn't give up. I worked hard to try and fit both full-time parenting in and full-time writing. I'd just begun to get myself into a good routine, writing every day and making good progress to revitalise my career, when I had another tiny human. I also expected this one, but once more I didn't quite understand how much my life and career were going to be interrupted for a second time.

You may be wondering how all that is relevant in a book about creating lots and not being a flake, but that's where I'm leading. In order to resuscitate my career for a second time and keep two tiny humans alive, I've developed many different techniques and tricks to get the most out of my worktime and my ability to write.

This book is about all the different elements of creating that aren't covered by knowing the basic craft of writing or marketing. This book is about working quicker. Making realistic goals, routines, rituals, and finding motivation. It's about celebrations and rewards. The carrot and the stick. It's about the actual process behind working, and getting the work done on difficult days, and good ones alike.

But mostly it's about one parent's journey of

learning how to not be a flake and actually get the job done.

Despite that, I hope there can be many relevant elements to this book for people who haven't got children, have grown up children, or who've also recently had something happen in life that makes them realise they need to become more serious, or make the time they have work harder for them.

Kids were my trigger point, but they don't have to be yours. This book can still help you make the most of your time and career.

If you don't yet know a few basics about your creative process, you may find this isn't the perfect book for you. I've assumed you have some basic understanding of how you write, how fast you are, who needs to be involved and how your time is divided.

I'll talk a little about ways to harness natural traits, but mostly this book is about strategy. It's about taming that muse and sticking a harness on it. It's about being a writer on your terms. It's about showing up, day after day. But it's also about fun. A sense of adventure. And most of all, about getting those wonderful characters, stories, universes and situations down onto paper for some other person to read, enjoy and relate to.

PREPARATION

This first section of the book can be considered the Preparation section. The bit where we talk about some of the stuff you need to do to literally prepare yourself to write. This is the section of lots of Ds. Dreams and Goals, Deadlines, Discipline. And Initiative and Organisation.

You can decide you're going to write a book, paint a picture, put together a song, or anything creative, but without all of the previously mentioned things, you won't be able to take it from the idea in your head all the way to completion or push through the harder bits. There's more to creativity than sitting down and thinking.

This section is where we talk about what you're actually trying to achieve—your dreams and goals—so you don't start going off in the wrong direction. If you want to work up to a movie deal, it's not going to make sense writing erotica shorts. If you want a series to come back to again and again, you probably don't want to be writing romance where each book sees those characters at their happy ending never to be written about again.

Then we'll touch a little on the planning and attitude side of things. You need to have milestones on the way to goals, and hitting those milestones should have some weight to it. And most importantly, you need to finish projects. If you don't finish something, you're not going to have something to sell or give to fans. And that means pushing yourself to see a project through. Discipline.

Finally, in this section I'll talk a little bit about Initiative and Organisation. I've found quite a few little things that can add up to making a big difference when it comes to being organised. And there are a million and one different ways of being organised. There are also a million and one little things you're going to need to know, especially if you go the indie route. You'll need to find your answers or the professionals with the answers yourself.

But, so I don't overwhelm you, let's go back to the beginning. I'm assuming you're reading this book because you want to create something. But something is pretty broad. So let's talk about your Dreams and Goals.

DREAMS AND GOALS

Everything we do in life begins with a dream. Most writers dream of telling that one story that matters, or of getting that bestseller. Some dream of a movie deal, and most writers love the idea of fan mail and glowing reviews for the brainchild they've created. Others still dream of having a lot of money from writing books.

They want to sell a million books, make ten grand a month. Get a publisher to put this series in this particular country. Or have audiobooks read by a celebrity they love. There are a lot of different dreams in this field of work, but they tend to all have one thing in common. They're largely out of our control.

Goals, however, are things we control. You can't directly control if someone is going to buy your book, offer you a movie deal or tell someone else, or you, how wonderful your words are. You can't control the celebrity you want for your audio book.

They might not like your genre, or be free that week.

Instead, you need to think about your dream as a sort of end result. And ask yourself what you can control that would get you closer to it. You might not be able to directly ask your celebrity to narrate your audio book, but they might do work for a particular audio book house, and that house might have a particular sales figure they like to see before they take on a book. Knowing all that can help you decide to market to the people in the right circles.

Other things you can control on a basic level are how many words you write. How good those words are. Your covers (if you're indie), and things like that.

So take your dream, whatever it is, and break it down into steps towards that dream, until you get to a goal—something you control. Let me go through my own dreams and goals as an example.

My dream is to be an author selling a million books per year and seeing some of those books made into TV series or movies. I'd also really like James Marsters to one day do the audio books for a particular series.

But my goal is always writing—and publishing—based. My biggest and most ambitious goal to date is publishing 20 books in 2020. This is a goal, not a dream, because I'm in direct control of publishing books as an indie author.

But let's go back to some smaller goals first. A goal I've achieved.

There's a yearly writer competition called NaNoWriMo—National Novel Writing Month. It challenges those entering to write 50k words in a single month, November, every year. I love it, and did it the first year I heard about it.

The first time I had a kid, I didn't do NaNoWriMo. It was the first year in 6 that I didn't even attempt it. And I'd won all of the previous five, my word count of the last of those a little over 60k. The next year, I managed to post an 85k NaNo with a kid. I was partially fuelled by how awful I'd felt not competing for a year, partially fuelled by the story I was writing, but I was mostly fuelled by some of the early techniques in this book.

I wanted to do NaNo with a small child. I knew it wasn't going to be easy, and there were a lot of elements I couldn't control, but I did have some I could. I plotted out the book a little more, and kept reading over my notes. I also asked a friend to take my child out for a morning once that month, and my fella did the same a few other mornings.

Once I knew exactly how much time I had, I worked out how much I could write per hour based on the previous months' word count per hour, and then multiplied it up. I then took off 20% for rough days, unexplained kid issues eating into my time, and stuff like that. That year I ideally needed 100k, but my figure came out more like 75k. I decided one would be my minimum goal and the other my maximum, and then I worked it out per day based on the hours I knew I had to work in. Each day I pushed myself to get the minimum. On good days I would push a little harder to hit the maximum. When a day fell apart, I made sure I had 500 words before I gave up.

By the end of the month I had 82.3k. I was ecstatic. I'd taken a realistic goal, a stretch goal, and fallen nicely in between. And I'd boosted my confidence, not only in my abilities, but my sense of what was a good goal.

Another two years on, I have another child, I've done two more NaNos (50k, right after my second was born, and 107k a year later, if you're curious). They've brought me to my current place of goal-setting, my 2020 goal of publishing 20 books. Let's go through how I set this goal.

I wanted to sell lots of books. I was also pretty broke at the time of making these goals from these dreams, so I couldn't just throw money at marketing the books I already had. That meant more books. The more books I have that are published, the easier and more effective marketing becomes, because every new hardcore fan buys more books before they've exhausted my back list.

This means the single best goal I can have to further my dream is to write and publish more books. How many books? I like my goals to be ambitious, but not insane, so I used my word count per hour of writing and multiplied that by half the time in a week I have available to work on my career. Why half? The other half is for edits, marketing, newsletters, and a little spare for the shit to hit the fan (something always goes wrong).

The maths leads me to knowing I can do about 20 books in one year, especially with a few extras I've got hoarded already.

20 books in one year is huge, however. And overwhelming and scary. And when I think about that alone I want to cry or run away, or eat my weight in chocolate buttons. But we're beginning to break

our dreams down into possible goals. If I just wrote any old twenty books and didn't think about anything else at all, it might well be a bit of a waste.

The first step has begun, however. After that, it's time to think about the strategy for those 20 books. Let's not worry about how easy they are or aren't to write yet. Let's think about which 20 books would be most strategic.

I already know that series of books sell well. I also already have fan bases in three genres—sci-fi, fantasy and dark romance, the latter of which is under a penname. It would make sense for my long-term success to give all my fans something in the year, and at regular intervals throughout it. If I break that down, goal-wise, I now have 6-7 books for each genre, and preferably at least some of them in a series.

Now that doesn't feel quite so overwhelming, does it? 6-7 books in a single genre, preferably in the same or a similar series. I'd already got two sci-fi standalones partly done. And I had a great idea for a 5-book space-pirates series. I didn't even need to think of new material for this genre. And see, we've identified, and in some cases, executed mini goals along the way.

So far our goal has gone like this.

20 books → 7 sci-fi books → one series and two part-stories to complete.

One of the sci-fi books already partway through, I was handwriting. Just a page a day. Writing a 250-300-word page of a book each day for a while no longer feels scary at all. Finally, I have an almost finished sci-fi short too. It could be another reader magnet and loss leader. It's written, and edited, just needs a proof and formatting. So my "7 books in sci-fi" goal is now a much less scary "one series and finish a handwritten book." I can do that.

From there we can move onto the fantasy element of the big goal. There's already one fantasy series. I have a fantasy epic already written, and 4 sequels planned for subsequent years. I also had the beginnings of another series with shorter-length books I excitedly plotted last year. I've been getting the character art, and need to write this for my Patreon readers anyway. Going a bit faster won't do me any harm. Add some of those books to the goals list and I'm most of the way there. That's book one of epic fantasy, then, and at least three for the series.

If I then also add in the usual Christmas stories I'll enjoy writing later in the year, the penname books (about 5 of those too), and another short or two that will take me by surprise at some point during the year, I've got all three genres handled. This will probably bring me to my 20: 7 sci-fi, 4 fantasy, 5 dark romance, 2 Christmas stories and 2 spares.

Now I could be very restrictive here if I wanted to be and plan out the exact 20, but I like a little extra leeway and some scope for my mind to change partway through the year. Over time you'll get an idea of how rigidly you need to treat it all. Or if you also need a little grace for extra projects that jump out at you.

I'd like to make a slight aside here to say these goals can be reached faster by sticking to one genre, but I've got a section later that talks about why I personally don't stick to a single genre and why you might not want to either.

Finally, I break all this down further, as we're still talking in books which can take months to complete. When planning my goals, I like to assign each book a word count. Some shorter, some longer. This gets easier with practice. If you're new to this, I'd consider adding ten percent to your first estimate just to be on the safe side. Most of the time I fall within that range. I almost always go slightly over, but by less and less these days.

For the 20 books I have coming out next year, the word count is shaping up to be approximately one million words. Thankfully I don't need to write that all in one year. I've been hoarding books, as I already mentioned. But if I did, I'd consider that to be just under 3k words per day, and that's what I'd aim for each day on average. My very last step is then to break that down week by week and day by day. Obviously, some days are going to yield better results than others.

In my case, one day a week I don't have both tiny humans. They have four hours of childcare on a Monday. That's four hours more for me to write.

In 2020 I'm actually aiming to write 2k words per day. This enables me to finish the books I want for 2020 on time and get the first set of books ready for 2021. 2k a day is an easy amount for me when I just have that to think about. You don't have to write every single day if you don't want to. I'll talk more about that in a later section as well. The important thing it to work out what you need to do each time you decide to write. What are your short-term, day-to-day goals?

With this process I kill the fear before it's even begun and stop procrastination in its tracks. Your daily goal shouldn't be scary the majority of the time. Some days, when the world seems to hate you and your tiny human has thrown up on you for the umpteenth time, and you're out of milk, and the car won't start, etc., any goal is scary. But when sat down in your favourite writing place with a drink you love and the rest of the day stretched before you, it should be more than doable.

And this can also work for less high-volume-based goals. If your dream is to be traditionally published, your first step could be getting an agent. You'd then break that down to finding the right agents to apply to, sending off X emails or queries.

If your dream is more simple, which is nothing to be ashamed of, say something like seeing a selection of your best poems in print, you could spend X amount of time each day choosing those, Y amount polishing them, then you'd need to decide on the order. Etc.

Whatever your dream, work out the first step towards it, then break that down into a goal you can control, and keep going.

I've got a small worksheet linked in the resources at the back of this book that you can use to help you work out goals and dreams.

Summary:

- You start by working out your dream.
- And then what you can control to get you closer.
- Then you strategize based on hours, ability,

external factors, etc. (more about that in later posts/chapters).

- Then you set realistic but challenging goals that will get those dreams a bit closer.

- Finally, you break those goals down to the day-to-day requirements that allow you to focus on a single task at once.

Quick Example:

- Dream: A million books sold in a certain timespan.

- What I can control: Write more books and publish them.

- Strategy: 20 books in 2020, 7 sci-fi (5 in one series), 5 penname books, 3 in bestselling series, and 2 establishing another series better. 4 fantasy books, two Christmas books and two spares to use when inspiration hits. After that, one book every 4 weeks, alternating between the 3 genres and the two series in each.

- Goal: Write 730k words minimum per year to maintain the schedule going forward. This will require about a thousand hours throughout the year. 500 for the writing and plotting, and another 500 for everything else. Leaving me some time to podcast. Just about doable. Going to be tough during preschool holidays, but easy during schooltime.

- Day to day: Write 2k words minimum. Do other tasks as needed and fit on top.

DEADLINES

Once you've set your goals and decided when you want your books to come out, you've only won some of the battle. Next you need to actually apply yourself and make it happen.

I think one of the biggest things that changed when I decided to take my writing career seriously was my attitude to my deadlines. As a self-employed anything, it's easy to think that because a lot of the deadlines are self-imposed, they're not important, but they are. Not just for your own sense of personal achievement, but also for being able to promise to fans or people within your line of work what will be delivered when.

I'd argue that respecting deadlines is more important than most realise. And personally, I find hitting them a lot more satisfying. Because I know I did it all by myself.

Douglas Adams famously said, "I love deadlines. I like the whooshing sound they make as they fly by."

I'm not like Douglas Adams, and I'd strongly suggest not being like him either. Deadlines are something I like to try and take more literally. The line at which point something will die if it goes over. Admittedly, I am naturally inclined this way, but if you're not, there are some ways to help yourself.

For some people, not letting their fans down can be a great motivator. It can actually be really helpful to empathise with their reaction if your project is late. How much will they hate you if you're late? How much will it damage your career if you don't get something done? It's a bit of a fearful way to approach something that shouldn't be a cause of stress, but it works for some. Think of it as the stick element of working to deadlines. Some people like the stick approach.

Other people use the Amazon pre-order as a way of helping turn deadlines into something tangible. The final version of the eBook must be uploaded three days before the book goes live or you risk losing pre-order privileges for a year. It also means more fans will be disappointed, and probably on a greater level, if the book is pushed back or cancelled. This can make a deadline a very real thing.

Also if a part of your marketing strategy relies on pre-orders, losing the privilege for a year can seriously hurt your bottom line. It takes the possibility of keeping your series readers going from series book to series book with no break away. They can't pre-order the next book if you've lost that ability. And some of those will forget your books while they wait.

Personally, I find that this is far too stressful. I

have young children and sometimes something beyond my control happens at the last minute. There are also plenty of other reasons this approach might not be for you. I can't imagine it can be a good idea if you have other commitments, health issues, or anything unpredictable in your life.

Here's a place balance comes in, and knowing yourself. I have decided that I don't want to run the risk of losing an important tool, so I don't put up a pre-order for a book unless it's written. But I have been putting my publishing schedule up on social media on a regular basis. This is a gentler way of dangling a stick over my head. I don't want upset fans, but it's not set in stone either—just my expected release schedule. They know as I get closer to a release, I will confirm it.

For the carrot side of deadlines, take a look at the rewards and celebrations section. If you stick to your deadlines, there's all sorts of ways to reward yourself. They can be a great tool while you're getting used to respecting deadlines more, and if you're more of a carrot person, they can be the best way to help you get the hardest elements of deadlines done, the tough bits that feel shit to have to wade through.

There's also a power and an emotional shift to being confident enough to say, "This is what I will do," on top of the accountability. You're declaring your intent to do something. That act alone can make the result more likely. Confidence in ourselves is huge when it comes to setting realistic deadlines.

Which brings me to the next point and the other element to setting deadlines. Realism. Your deadlines need to be sensible.

Knowing what you're capable of and having a positive but realistic attitude to your limits is important when you decide what the initial deadlines are. It's no good deciding that you must get books X, Y, and Z out all in the same month if it means you've got to write five times your average for the next three months to get them written on time. It will burn you out. Deadlines need to take into account a pacing that you're happy with.

You need to know how quickly you can write, and what else is going on in your life. We all need holidays, and we all get sick occasionally. Work in some wriggle room. Not so you can play games or watch TV or procrastinate until the schedule is as tight as possible, but so you can get sick, be there for a friend or child, or survive that important meeting you'd forgotten about.

So work out what realistic amount you can write per week or month, then make deadlines based on that.

On top of that, I like to set a first-draft soft deadline six months before the publishing date, and a hard deadline three months before the publishing date. This helps me get a handle on which books need to be done when. It gives me a place to work from. Soft deadlines are something to aim for. Hard deadlines are something to work through the night to meet. Ideally you will then find you bounce around your soft deadlines, never getting too close to the hard ones, but equally unlikely to be ahead of your soft deadlines unless you've had a really good writing patch.

It helps me feel like I can catch up without too

much effort if I'm only behind on a soft deadline. If I'm aiming for my soft deadline and I'm a week late, I'm still twelve weeks ahead of my hard deadline. And catching up a week's worth of work over the next twelve weeks isn't insurmountable. That helps me to be calm but focused.

Finally, I also find it really helpful to think about who is needed as part of each goal. Books aren't solo projects, despite the idea we have internalized, of lonely writers holed up in cabins in the woods. You need to factor in the rest of the team. Editor, formatter, cover designer, etc. Even if they're you, as well.

If your cover designer requires three months' notice for a cover, then you need to have told them in plenty of time that the book is on the way. And if your editor needs a couple of weeks to edit your book, then you need to factor that in as well.

With something like a book there's more than one deadline. The writing is just one part of the plan. It can help to set deadlines for each part of the process, essentially breaking down your goals into even smaller parts. And this also has the extra added benefit of making them seem less overwhelming.

I often like to use a spreadsheet, and then I plug in the date I want to publish. In the next column over, I subtract the number of days I need to format, then the next column I subtract the number of days for a final draft, the next the days my editor takes (with an extra ten percent margin), the next how much warning my editor needs to edit a book, and the next column I subtract my time for a second draft (often with a little margin too). This gives me a deadline for the first draft that is fairly inflexible. Then I add my soft deadlines in, three months before that. I've included a basic spreadsheet template at the end of the book if you'd like an idea of how I do it.

I know deadlines aren't everyone's cup of tea. They add a lot of stress to some people's lives, but with the right balance of realism and optimism they can be a very powerful tool. And they make you seem—and feel—more professional. When it all comes down to it, however, you need to decide how much it all matters to you. Nothing motivates a person to work as well as passion does.

But my biggest piece of advice is to stick to deadlines like you are taking them literally. Your satisfaction is worth it alone.

Summary:

- Make a list of your publishing dates for whatever period you're planning.
- Work out the other elements of the process.
- List them in reverse order.
- Get your hard deadline for the first draft.
- Optional step: decide on a soft deadline.
- Calculate how long you have to write each book.
- Estimated task or word count/days to do it = daily workload to stay on schedule.
- See if this marries up to your pacing estimates.
- Decide if you need to adjust anything to bring

down the task from 'insane' to just 'challenging'.

Example:

- Publishing dates: A book every 4 weeks from Jan 2nd 2021.

- Other elements: Books need formatting, editing, final-drafting and second-drafting time, as well as a cover and plotting time.

- In reverse order: Cover for print, formatting, final draft, cover for eBook, editing, second draft.

- Hard deadlines: Three months for all the above added together, so first book written by Oct 2nd 2020, then +4 weeks for each book thereafter.

- Soft Deadlines: I add three months to the timeframe, so my first book needs to be written by July 2nd 2020, then +4 weeks for each book thereafter.

- How long calculation: My penname books are shorter, fantasy next length, and then sci-fi, but 12 weeks for one of each (approx. 165k). That's 15,750 per week, 2250 per day. Not a huge amount.

- Previous pacing: 2k per day with time in a month to format, commission covers and final draft, one day on top per month each. Second draft, one week per month on top. So I just need to fit in another 250 words per day.

- Do I need to adjust the deadlines? Probably

not. It's such a small amount extra that with practice and the occasional late night I should be able to stay on top of the deadlines.

DISCIPLINE AND INITIATIVE

I know what you're thinking, didn't we just talk about being disciplined? Isn't that what making deadlines is? Well, yes, and no, and sort of.

Hitting deadlines can be done in two ways. You can pretend it doesn't exist and do something else (often anything else), until you're not sure it's quite possible to hit the deadline anymore, and then create in a mad rush. Some people seem to genuinely enjoy creating in this way. Or you can chip away at your project bit by bit, day by day, until it's done.

For stress levels, for predictability, and for resilience against unforeseen circumstances, I recommend the latter. I used to create as and when, and then I had children and found that not only do they eat into your time randomly, and without warning, but they don't appreciate you having deadlines either.

I found that the best combat to being interrupted and derailed by the stressors of life is to develop a disciplined habit of some kind. For me, I find writing every single day is the best way. I keep track of how many uninterrupted days in a row I write. I will hit 1000 on May 4th 2020. This is part of being disciplined. I make myself sit down and write.

This is probably one of the hardest elements to explain. How do I do that? How do you make yourself do something? Well, for me, I ask myself how badly I want something. I've got an 850+ writing-day streak. I know I'm going to be gutted if I break that streak. So on the worst of days, I do 500 words. And then if I still feel awful, I give up for the day.

What I've noticed is that most days, however, pushing myself to do the 500 gets me back in the right frame of mind, and with the habit forming over time, it gets easier. This kind of muscle is always hardest to exercise at the beginning. And you should almost expect to fail. It took six years of trying to develop a daily habit before I hit the current stride. But each time I tried I got better at it, closer. Until it finally stuck. Discipline is a muscle just like any other. It requires training.

You don't have to do this, and I'll talk more about routine later in the writing section, but you don't have a boss, so you are the only person who is going to make you sit down and get on with something day after day. There are things you can do to help with this, and that's where your goals and dreams come in. Your dreams are your reason why.

I've found it helpful now and then to think about my dreams and the goals to get there and remind myself why I'm pushing hard, and what for. It's also apparently a big psychological boost to visualise the dream you're aiming for. It gives you a boost as if you've actually been experiencing it, and then you're in a better space to create.

It also helps you remember why you care, because sadly, others won't. Not as much as you do. Some people might care about you enough to want to see you happy. But they won't care enough about exactly how to put in the effort for you. And they shouldn't. Dean Wesley Smith has said in many of his presentations that one of the most freeing things to remember is that no one else cares.

No one cares—so you have to. No one else cares, so you can do exactly what matters most to you. And no one else cares if you fail or not. You don't even need to tell most people. You can dust yourself off and carry on again. Or set a new goal, or a new dream. As long as you're getting yourself closer to something that makes you happy and achieve something, you'll get there.

Discipline is also one of those things where you decide how much, too. Your goals and dreams have whatever timeframe you've set on them. That means you are the final decision-maker in how disciplined you actually need to be. Of course, being patient doesn't come naturally to most people, so you'll need to weigh that up as you work towards your goal.

I also sometimes challenge myself to get to a goal quicker. Just to see if it's possible. Some of my great leaps forward in productivity have come from doing NaNoWriMo each year. I always set two goals. My baseline needed amount, and an amount that is a little over the previous year. And then I see how disciplined I can be.

Each year I've done better than I expected. And each year I've taken my writing speed and efficiency up a notch. Discipline also gets easier with time and practice, which links into another chapter a bit later. Discipline is the beginning stage. It's what you need to use to get into good habits, and on bad days when you've got nothing else.

Most importantly, it's one of the major things that prevents your being a flake. It's easy to get excited about an idea when it's all shiny and new, but after time that fades. What's left is the hard graft and the results needed to put food on the table.

This is especially important if you're collaborating. Someone else is relying on you to get what needs doing done, so you can't flake out on them. At least, not easily.

I also think initiative goes hand in hand with discipline. It's very easy to look at a goal, realize you don't know how to do an element, and then wait for someone to teach you or explain it to you. But as I've already mentioned before, no one else cares about your reaching your dream anywhere near as much as you do.

When it comes to making progress, to learning how to be better at your craft, or needing to solve some kind of problem along the way, you need to show initiative. There's almost no problem under the sun that can't be solved with an internet search or the right question in the right place on social media. Or a book. There's a lot of good books out there.

Taking initiative doesn't mean going it alone all the time, however. It just means having a different attitude when you come up against a problem. It means putting the responsibility to do something about each problem on your own shoulders. And discipline means doing it without too much delay, even when you feel a little bored, annoyed, or possibly even embarrassed for asking a question.

Life isn't always easy. Shit happens. Sometimes that shit is career-related, and sometimes it isn't, but a little bit of progress, one way or another, day after day, can soon add up. And there's a certain pride you can take in pushing onwards towards your goals on the hard days. Even if you only make a little progress. You build a sort of confidence out of the discipline and initiative until the average not-so-good day doesn't stop you at all.

I've had a few shit-happens moments recently. Back in May last year my mother was taken very ill suddenly, and was rushed to hospital. She was so unwell I had to drop everything and travel through the night to the other side of the country. Most of the journey there I struggled to keep my eyes open, but I couldn't do much for a few hours once I got there. There was a brief moment after I arrived at my brother's house to stay when I felt more awake for the sudden conversation with his partner and the plan-making for the morning, and I was pretty worried on top. I couldn't sleep, and I couldn't go see my mum yet, so I pulled out my laptop and I did a little writing.

My brain wasn't really in the best of writing moods, but I knew I had a Christmas story that needed writing. And Christmas was far enough removed from life that writing it didn't seem so hard. I quickly jotted down a few basic plot notes for the idea I'd already had, and then wrote blind, not sure about anything but my need for a distraction. I managed about 600 words before sleep caught up with me and I crashed.

The next day I wrote another 800 words on a mix of my phone while being driven to and from the hospital, and once more after I got back to my brother's before I crashed again. For the next three or four days, that was all I could manage. A few hundred words tapped out here and there in a story that didn't matter that much.

My mother made a full recovery despite battling for her life during the illness, and I eventually finished the story and started a series that's now signed to a wonderful publisher and has probably been the biggest contract signing of my career so far. That one little decision when I got there, to write something to take my mind off difficult things and then to just keep going, little by little, has led to my best career opportunity to date. The book turned into a series, and the five-book series was snapped up, through a roundabout route, by Anthem Press, under the care of one of the biggest sci-fi authors currently out there.

Shit happens, but not giving up can sometimes be the beginning of something phenomenal.

Finally, there's something very satisfying about achieving something hard. Or reaching a dream that once seemed impossible. There's nothing like an achievement being hard for making the result satisfying. If you've set big goals, and you have to really work for them, when they happen they make you feel phenomenal. And they also build your confidence to tackle more things in the future.

You just need to find the right balance. Your goals and milestones need to be high enough that you make satisfying progress, and low enough that you don't overwhelm yourself. Experiment and find what works for you.

Summary:

- Take your goals and push yourself to work towards them a little every day.

- If you encounter a problem, find someone or something to help you get past it.

- Experiment with different types and scopes of challenge.

Example:

- I write every day, and don't let myself take a day off writing at least 500 words.

- If something goes wrong, I ask on Discord, social media or google for the answer. If it's an emotional problem, I have three friends I go to (depending on the problem) for emotional support. Otherwise I'll find a how-to guide or an appropriate expert in a Facebook group, or blog or podcast setting.

- I've learnt that I need to compete with my previous years' results, so I track my word counts and progress and try to beat them. I also know I need to get off to a good start each month, so I schedule very little for the first week and keep it free for writing.

ORGANISATION

Now I'm sure you've all heard this one before. Being organised makes things easier to achieve. And I'm sure by now you're probably all almost sick of everyone telling you that you need to be organised before telling you exactly how to do it (usually their way).

And to some degree, yes, that is exactly what I'm about to do. But, I'm going to do it with one caveat: everyone is different. That means the best way for you to be organised is different. And there may be times in your life where one method works better than another, and then life changes and so what works best changes too.

Before I had tiny humans, I never needed a to-do list. I remembered everything. And I truly mean it. I almost never forgot a single thing, and even if I forgot something for a while, I remembered it in time to do something about whatever it was.

Now I've had tiny humans there is a lot more to

remember, and I need to change focus partway through a day. Although I still remember pretty much everything I need to, there's a time requirement to go from thinking about family-related tasks to thinking about writing-related tasks. Having some organisation, in my case a bullet journal, helps me switch from one mode to the other far, far quicker.

So, let's talk a little about to-do lists and bullet journals.

A few people I know swear by to-do lists. And they can be useful, but studies have shown that for a lot of people to-do lists cause as much anxiety as they fix. The reason for this is the flawed nature of human beings. We have a tendency when making to-do lists of sticking everything we can think of on one, regardless of the actual necessity or how crucial it is to do that task.

While there's a certain amount of satisfaction from making a list and ticking some easy early tasks off, what often happens is a few tasks linger. Some of these tasks are ones that actually don't matter, or turn out to be problems solved in other ways. Some of these tasks are actually too large, and should be broken down. What ends up happening therefore is a to-do list that never quite gets done. And those last few tasks can either pressure us into finishing stuff we shouldn't (because we don't need to, or need to go about it in a different way), or make us feel anxious and unsatisfied because we never completed the list.

There are apps that solve this problem, allowing stuff to be rescheduled and deleted and hiding tasks until it's the right time for them. And there's bullet journaling. Bullet journaling is a wonderful process that does a similar thing, but it also allows you to do it by hand. It's organisation without quite so much overwhelm because you move on if you're sick of the current list, and the process of using it naturally encourages this.

It's also designed to be both pretty and functional, although I'd strongly recommend not worrying too much about how fancy it is. Functional works well. The pretty stuff can often be an unnecessary time-sink. I quickly colour in boxes if I need to, but otherwise pretty much everything is standard ticks and crosses. I know many people who do funky things with Washi tape, however. And the official bullet journal website has many other ideas.

But the general gist of it is to make yourself a longer-term page (I like doing 6 months across a double page), where you add in the big events. For me that's birthdays, days when I don't have the usual childcare, and publication days for my books. If I have holidays, dentist's visits or anything else I know a long time in advance, I might put those in here too. But you should put the stuff in there that you need most.

Then, at the beginning of each month, I take another double-page spread, and on the left-hand side I number down for the days. I then add in that month's birthdays, events and publication dates from my six-month spread. Once I've done that, I add in my recurring tasks. Posting to Patreon, newsletters, podcasts, and anything else I know will happen with regularity.

I've also trialled writing my word count goals here and the books they match with, but I found it got too messy. Instead, I now use a cheap paper calendar for that, and I write in pencil so I can recalculate if I need to. I'm trying to switch this over to a spreadsheet, but I might switch back. I like having stuff by hand; it goes into my brain better. This is again something that you need to trial for yourself. How you lay it out can make a huge difference. It needs to be something you can look at and understand quickly, and at the same time be comprehensive but not overwhelming.

Finally, for the month, I write the tasks I need to do for sure on the right-hand page, starting with monthly tasks that I can just copy from the previous month. Things like finances (I like doing this monthly so my end of year isn't awful), newsletter planning, Patreon rewards, etc. Then I add in the writing I want to do as a monthly whole. Finish writing X book, do edits on Y book. Commission cover for Z book. Format a book for print, etc.

Then I add in entirely one-off tasks I know I need to do at some point during the month. I also add tasks here at a later date if they come up and if I know I need to do them that month, but not right away. Like sort a tax form for someone, or message someone about something.

Then I have a day list on the next spare page. These are much more condensed. I head them with the date and day, then I add recurring stuff in. I have boxes to make sure I drink enough. A box to check in with my Discord (Discord is a messaging system designed for gamers but well adapted to writers—it even has a sprint bot). And then my to-write item, my second-drafting item. And anything else I think will fit into that single day.

Each new day, month and six-month period, I essentially start again, making a new list. Items naturally don't get done. Anything left at the end of the day is either ignored because I decide it doesn't matter as much as I thought, rescheduled, or, because it turns out the task is too big, broken down into smaller tasks to work into subsequent days.

Now, you might not need all of these things. You might need other things. I forget to drink enough, and I like to write every single day. You might not move around too much and want to track your steps, or you might like to do social media every day.

The great thing about a bullet journal is you can change your mind too, and you can use any kind of journal. There are official guided ones, but the options are so limitless it's all down to your own needs. Mostly because the nature of it is to start again the next day, month, or whatever time frame you work off, you can structure it differently the next day if you need to.

I have a friend who writes her to-do lists on post it notes. Each item on a single post it, with a few details if the task is huge. She then sticks them to the wall beside her desk. When they're done, she pulls them off. If they fall off because they've been there so long and she's not done them, she decides whether that task can just go in the bin or if it needs to be rewritten and stuck back on. (They usually go in the bin.)

Another friend uses a whiteboard and boxes, and moves stuff around. There are literally a thousand different ways you can organise your tasks. You just need to make sure there's a way for tasks that aren't the right fit for your goals and dreams to fall off (literally or figuratively).

When you do, this will also need to be something you test. I tried to do this in the morning for a while, but I was constantly interrupted by children and I would lose my train of thought. Instead, it's now the last thing I do in the evening before bed.

And I even sleep better. I essentially empty my worries and anxiety about all the things I have to do onto the page right before I go to bed, and I don't come back to them the following day until I'm ready to. And because I know when my reliable hours to work are, I can come back to it knowing that in the meantime there's nothing I need to do. So I also enjoy time with my kids more.

However, I have friends who find this keeps them up at night. The very act of thinking about what they need to do and beginning the process of planning when to do it then means they can't stop thinking about it, and they lie awake fretting. Instead, they like to make a list just for that single day when they first sit down. They're a little more likely to forget a task, but equally they can sleep at night.

You'll need to work out a system that gives you the best capacity to remember everything, balanced with the right time of day and method to reduce overwhelm. And then evolve it as needed to get to each of your next milestones.

Summary:
- Find a type of to-do list or organisation system that works for you.

- Adapt this to your specific goals.
- Work it into your daily life at the best moment.
- Stress less.

Example:

- I take the basic bullet journal model with six months, monthly and daily sections.
- Then I add some project sections, newsletter-planning sections and a book-release schedule.
- I don't go to bed without working out the next day's list.
- Then I can forget about it when not working.

HURDLES

So far, I've talked about how you can begin to prepare yourself more easily and effectively, but there are a few other things I'd like to talk about before we get to the actual creation section.

There are quite a few different elements to actually creating, and there are quite a few emotional elements linked to that. And I suppose that's really where this section focuses. What's going on in a writer's head. It's a big jumble of thoughts, worries, fears, hopes, and everything we've ever experienced and been taught. Then you add in our characters and the universes they live in on top, and it's a pretty crazy place.

And it can be a pretty lonely, isolating place. It's easy to feel misunderstood, or hopeless, when shit happens. It's easy to wonder if it is all worth it. Or worry that what we've just created totally sucks and is the suckiest piece of sucky writing in the history of sucking.

These thoughts, worries and baggage we have from previous failures can trip us up and prevent us from even sitting down to write, or sabotage us on the first words alone. It can cause havoc.

This section deals with how you can handle your emotions and mentality relative to your feelings. It explores ways you can learn to cope. What thoughts you can ignore, and when you just need someone else to tell you what you can't seem to tell yourself.

I'm also going to talk about procrastination. Let's face it, no book on productivity would be complete without something on procrastination. Everyone does it. I've even done it writing this book. When it comes to working on anything, procrastination always pops up at some point. But it's something that can be tamed and overcome. Beating procrastination is just another skill. And just like other skills, it can be learnt and applied again and again.

Finally, although writers tend to have moments where they combat these things, it's easier, and the downs in life are less difficult if the writer knows how to communicate effectively with others and build the right network of accountability and support around themselves. We all have bad days, but the right friends can help bring us out of creative lows and put us back into the creative zone again.

So let's start with what goes on inside our heads.

Emotions, Procrastination and Positivity

Emotions:

Telling a story with empathy and depth requires a person to have an understanding of emotions and their different extremes. I think this naturally makes creative people feel more deeply. And we're used to pondering these feelings.

Quite a few people who are creative and have had some kind of therapy often express a slight fear that if they get too much better, they won't be able to create the breadth of pieces they wish because they won't understand the damaged elements of life as much. I know some of my best stories have taken an element of trauma I've personally been through and added it to a character's story. I can write those things so much more authentically, even if it takes a toll on my own emotional stability.

On top of that, I think writers have a natural curiosity for things that create deep feelings. We want to understand what it feels like to be an X kind of person, or to have Y happen to us. And it can make for an awful lot of emotions. We want to feel, and we need to feel to create well.

On the flip side of the emotional coin, I think creating can be emotional in and of itself. We have worries, fears, anxieties and all sorts over the craft, what others will think, if we've got this character right, or have we dealt with this important issue the right way. It's enough to keep the deepest sleeper awake at night, considering if they should change something somewhere in the hopes they'll have crafted the perfect story.

Part of being a good, consistent writer who isn't derailed by emotion is to learn to not let the emotional element overwhelm us. We can feel too much, all at once, and it can take time to calm back down.

I know earlier in my career it would sometimes take me weeks to write through a scene where something bad happened. And I'd need tissues. The first time I killed a character I cried so much. I was also easily blindsided and derailed by the emotions of others. My grandma died about five years ago, and for months I struggled to write anything.

Every time I tried to write any kind of scene, it came out wrong, not how I'd intended it. It was always darker or sadder, or just more hard work and uninteresting.

I tried to sum up how things turned out by saying it was like painting a picture where you go to use the normal colours you would for a particular scene, only to discover after you've added it to the page that someone has mixed black into the paint and the whole picture comes out darker, grungier and less appealing than you'd been intending. It took several months to process this and get back to creating properly. I let the emotions dictate what I was doing, and I wallowed in them.

For days I didn't create. Some days I would try. I would sit in front of the laptop and think about my story, and then about five minutes in, after I'd written about 7 words, I would declare myself done and hurting too much to want to write, and then I wouldn't try again for another week.

Months went by like this until someone reminded me that my grandma had loved my books and would have wanted me to keep making them. As I got back into it, the colours quickly returned to normal, but it took me pushing myself past the worst of the emotions and not dwelling on them.

There were still moments I felt sad. I still cry every Christmas Day for a moment when I remember that I would have phoned her in a particularly quiet section of the day, but it doesn't stop me writing.

Emotions are something to be harnessed a little, explored a little and experienced a little. We can't bottle them up, but equally we can't be ruled by them.

When we feel a particular emotion, any kind, be it anger, sadness, elation, excitement, etc., we need to give it a moment. Accept it. Our emotions are always valid, and always have a reason. If you know the reason, great, but if not, try to give yourself a moment to think why. You still might not work it out, but emotions shouldn't be bottled. There's a time and place for them. Bottling them will just freeze you up and make creativity with depth and passion harder. And it will take a good deal of your motivation along with it. The act of thinking about what caused the emotion will help you process it and decide if you should push past it, or allow it more time. And, as I've said elsewhere, be as honest with yourself as you can.

I've also talked about harnessing them. In some ways I think writers are master emotional manipulators. We spend our time crafting stories that take others on emotional journeys. If we can harness a story to make others feel something, we can do the same for ourselves.

When my emotions are holding me back, and I've gone through the process of deciding how and whether I want to push past them or not, if I do, I know I need to harness things a little. In this situation I seek something to literally make me feel excited about my goal again. This is usually celebration-related, but it can be a reward if I do something. Or a dream. Failing that, I'll remind myself of a past success, take a quick look at my own fan mail, or a bunch of other milestone markers, all of which I talk about a little more in a latter chapter.

In short, I take control of my inner dialogue and redirect it in the most helpful direction. I tell myself what I need to hear in my own way to get my emotions in a more helpful space. I'll also talk a bit more about that in the positivity section of this chapter, but for now, let's move on to something all people face.

Procrastination:

This is the very definition of being ruled by emotion. Sometimes we need to be honest with ourselves about this too! Is it our emotions stopping us, or actually something else?

I don't think anyone is lazy, ever. But people procrastinate for some very simple reasons.

Firstly, the tasks, goals or dreams they have are too large, and therefore overwhelming.

If this is why you're procrastinating, then it's time to go back to your goals and tasks, and break them down further. I've already talked a bit about this in previous chapters so I won't dwell on it too much here. But with practice you'll find the size of task that doesn't overwhelm you, but challenges you and helps grow you instead.

Sometimes I also procrastinate because I just don't know how to do a task. Remember, this also came up in the to-do list section. Sometimes a task isn't right for us because we don't yet know how to do it. Once, when I was in the early stages of my career and aware I needed a newsletter, I put "grow newsletter" on my list of goals.

I added it to the list one day. And I ignored it. Then it went on the next day. And I ignored that too. Weeks went by, before I gave myself a really good mental reprimand and got on with figuring out where to start. I should have put down something like, "research newsletter hosting sites" or "research ways to get readers to sign up." Or any of the other activities in the process that I could have begun with. And then there should have been a task to implement each of those elements.

Another reason I think we procrastinate is simply because something is really hard. If a challenge is too big, we can want to not tackle it. The solution to this is almost as simple as above. We've got to find a way to learn it. And that's where our initiative comes in. Once you've recognised that the task is something you don't understand how to do, you can use the internet, and other people, books, etc., to find out how.

There's barely any subject under the sun that doesn't have a YouTube video, a blog or a podcast about it these days. If you're putting off a task because you don't have the skills for it, find a way to learn. Or, if money isn't an issue, consider paying someone else to do it.

I remember the first time I was publishing a book myself. It was back in 2010 and there was a particular eBook website that allowed you to upload a file and it would convert it into all sorts of formats for all sorts of e-readers and send them out to major eBook retailers. Back when lots were on the market, and Kindle hadn't emerged as the dominant force.

The file had to be done in exactly the right way or the file converter threw a hissy fit like no other. And it had some quirks. But, after three weeks of me putting this task off because I had no clue where to begin, I gave myself a verbal reprimand, sat myself down and searched.

And for those wondering what a verbal reprimand is like, I don't do a lot. I'm not trying to beat myself up. More, I talk to myself in a motivational way, so I'll say something along the lines of, "Come on, chikka (my pet name for myself), time to get this done and off your mind. You'll feel better for it, and you've put it off long enough."

Then I did what I needed. It turned out the people who provided the service had a guide. And the guide was well put together and well explained. It covered everything I needed to know. Only about an hour later, I had a file ready to upload.

It went through first time, no problem. And I learnt a skill that's still with me today. I can now handle formatting in Word and LibreOffice in a way that makes my life so much easier. And I've helped out other authors who were stuck on more than one occasion. Now, when I get stuck on something, I don't take three weeks to go find the resource I need to learn, or the person I need to ask.

You do also need to balance this with knowing your limitations, though. I tried to tackle covers once. I pay a cover designer now. Every time. And I make sure that's a cost I prioritise. There was no amount of learning that was going to make it worth me doing that task myself.

The final reason I think we procrastinate is that the reward for the task is too disproportionately low compared to the effort we put in it. As I hinted at above, some tasks are not worth us fixing ourselves. And I think this is made worse when it comes to how much energy we have. If we're burnt out, in a bad space mental-health-wise, these tasks can become mountains, and we can end up pretending they don't exist.

While the to-do list set up to let tasks fall off has its benefits, it can mean these sorts of tasks simply don't get done. They fall off before we can summon up the motivation to do them.

I like to tackle these tasks a little differently. I attach a reward (something I'll talk about a bit more in another chapter) and a deadline if necessary, and I break them down into even smaller, regular tasks, an average smaller, bearable amount each day.

I hate second-drafting. It's something that only adds so much value to a finished book, but it has to be done if I want a decent product and my editor to be happy with me.

So I've broken it down. I second-draft 2-3 chapters 5 days a week. And I try to do it at a similar time of day too. I still don't enjoy it, but little by little, day by day, it gets done. And often, when I'm near to the end of a WIP, I can make progress a bit quicker. The end comes into sight and I can push myself over it. Sending it off to the editor is a great feeling. And I hang onto the memory of how that feels to help, which brings me to my next point in this chapter.

Sometimes if it's not got a deadline attached, but I can't keep putting off a big task, I just do as much as I can bear each day, not letting myself off the hook until I've done at least some.

I also do the difficult tasks first each day, and schedule a favourite activity right after. This can be another motivator in and of itself, a bit like a reward. After all, it works with kids and getting them to eat their veg. Promise them ice cream if they do!

Positivity:

There's a lot to be said for the power of positivity. I know this is something you've probably heard of before, but I want to make a small distinction. True positivity isn't pretending everything is okay when it's not. It's knowing some things aren't right or normal, or perfect, but choosing to focus on something else instead. As I've mentioned at the end of the Emotions section, it's taking control of the inner dialogue in your head and redirecting it to something more pleasant, something more positive, or something better for you.

Being positive about difficult situations is hard, but sometimes, being positive about easy things is just as hard. I've got a friend who can push on through the worst of moods and get the job done, and is then pleased with himself, but if he achieves something that he deems ought to be easy, he is almost grumpy about it, believing that, because it was easy, his completion of the task has very little merit. It doesn't matter to him that it's only easy because he's practiced that something more than others.

We need to make sure we give ourselves less of a hard time. When you've been writing for a while, some stuff is stuff you should know how to do, but we all learn different things at different paces, and we forget them at different rates too.

Creative careers are hard enough already without belittling ourselves and our capabilities.

On top of that, there's the more general, and frankly harder, in my opinion, positivity in difficult circumstances. I think this is a little similar to goal setting. When stuff is beyond your control, you have to let it go. And focus on something you can control.

When I had my second child, it threw my writing world into a tailspin. I thought I'd be a lot more prepared. I'd had one, and I knew how much writing meant to me. But nothing quite prepared me for how little sleep I'd be getting and what that would do to my mood. Or how clingy my little one would be.

I wanted to write so desperately, and struggled not to focus on how few words I was writing compared to the time before my baby had been born. But, after a few weeks, I sat down and worked out how many hours I was actually writing. Even doing some of it on my phone, instead of my laptop, I was writing about 10% more words per hour than I had been.

On one hand, I could look at my total words each day and be unhappy. On the other, I had done more per minute than ever before. Trying to be positive is focusing on the latter and then trying to work out ways to get more time.

With this mentality I got myself through NaNoWriMo that year. My youngest was only three weeks old when I started it. And I wrote about 90% of it on my phone, almost all while I was breastfeeding him. Some of it even at night, to help keep myself awake. Most days I didn't focus on my overall word count. I focused on the positive aspect. The writing speed. Even sleep-deprived and on the phone, it was still decent. And it showed me how effective I could be in just ten minutes.

I've carried that positivity forward, finding it gets easier naturally as you focus on the things that are good and work out how to make more of that happen. Now I can write over two thousand words per hour on average. That means it takes only 25 hours to do NaNo amounts over a month.

Over time I'm slowly growing faster, and I'm able to get into everything quicker. Given that at the very beginning of my career I used to write less than a quarter of the average I get now, it's a great thing to feel positive about.

Positivity is also handy when it comes to a lot of the other aspects of our career. It's very easy to let things like imposter syndrome derail something, or let a bit of criticism knock the wind from our sails, but we can't let that happen if we want to create lots. You have to push the negative aspects of those aside. And sometimes it has to come down to choosing to do so. Sometimes you have to choose to focus on how well you did one element to not let yourself get dragged down by how badly you did another.

But positivity is also not something that waits for perfection. Our writing will never be perfect. There will always be something we could have done better. Positivity is being happy with our best at any given moment, however.

My first book was so shockingly bad I had to unpublish it. But I also love my first book, and I'm super-proud of it. Because it was the best I could do then. Knowing it's badly written doesn't hurt or even bother me. It started my journey. It was my first stepping stone. Without it, and everything I learnt writing it, I'd not be where I am today, writing books I can genuinely be proud of and think are awesome.

Your best should always be good enough. And your best can vary. Your best when you've had a wonderful morning, the perfect breakfast and your muse is just handing you everything is not the same as your best when you have a screaming baby who has woken you every hour through the night and you can barely keep your eyes open, let alone worry about whether your plot makes sense or your characters' motivations are consistent.

To some degree, this is also where practice can come in. You'll have a better idea of what your best is when you've written plenty and when you've gone through the ups and downs of life while keeping your writing going. But the very base line of positivity, I think, is just not giving up. Holding on to some small spark and pushing yourself to deliver a little something each and every day, no matter how small.

With time, the muscles grow, and before you know it, you've got past successes to hang on to and remind yourself of as well.

I've got a few friends who also like having stuff on their walls to remind them of good things. Framed royalty checks, a bookshelf with all their printed books on. Markers for past achievements. Anything that helps you refocus on what you're trying to do and takes the positives from the journey you've already managed.

You can do this, one step at a time, until many steps lie behind you.

Summary:

- Your emotions are important. Validate them.

- Learn to be self-aware enough to recognise when you need to give them space or need to push them aside. Harness them.

- Identify procrastination and the reason behind it.

- Fix the reason as sensibly as you can.

- Push past the procrastination to the best of

your ability.

- Be careful what you focus on.
- Try to find the positive element of a situation or result.
- Measure progress in a way that helps you keep positive about your progress.

Example:

- When I was struggling because I miscarried, I identified the grief and stages of grief I was feeling.
- Each day I decided if it was something I needed to process, or if I needed to just give it more time. Sometimes I pushed the feelings aside, knowing I had to carry on for the sake of the child I already had. Sometimes I decided to do something to help me process my emotions, such as journaling, speaking to a therapist, or many other activities, like going for a walk, watching TV, etc.
- I was honest to myself about when I was actually just procrastinating and asked myself why.
- Once I'd identified if I was scared, overwhelmed, or didn't know how to do something, I fixed it as well as I could.
- And then I tried again as soon as possible.
- I try not to think about how much I could have got done, but the average words written per hour and the monthly and yearly word-

count totals.

- I keep track of each month and year in a long-term spreadsheet and try to beat my records.

Communication

This may seem like a funny chapter in a book about getting stuff done, but I think a lot of people underestimate the importance of this one. As writers and creators, it's very easy to get lost in our own heads. We get involved in the worlds of our characters and we don't remember the other stuff. While to-do lists can help with this a little, one of the big areas a lot of people lack is communication. Funny for a writer in some ways. You'd think we'd be good at this.

The first element I want to address is reading. And I don't mean reading books, although that's a great thing to do. I mean reading things like instructions, briefs and messages from other people. You'd be surprised how many writers suck at reading.

Recently a big indie author group on Facebook mentioned that they were starting to put together a new idea for bundling books of a genre and helping newer authors get a leg up in terms of visibility by adding some big-name authors to the mix. The instructions clearly asked people to find their genre in the comments and add a reply if they had a book in that genre. And only if they didn't find their genre to make a new comment for that genre.

In less than thirty minutes the admins of the group had shut comments off entirely because so many authors had just made new comments with their genre and not added their reply to others. It was chaos. It almost stopped the whole thing going ahead. And then when it came to submissions for the very first one, the admin had to ask people to follow the instructions so many times he just started rejecting books if the instructions weren't followed to the letter. If you're a writer, you need to make sure you're reading the messages, posts, emails, etc., correctly. You can lose out on important chances, or put off a potential mentor or helper by not doing so.

And the same goes for messages with people who might be working with you. If you have a publisher, or are trying to submit a book to one, you need to read emails carefully, give people the information they need the first time. Let your cover designer or your editor know what's going on and what you need from them. Try to avoid having a chain of emails as they ask you for every tiny detail you forgot. You don't want to waste their time or yours.

Good communication with others also helps to set expectations. You need to tell people what's going on. Give them ideas of what you're doing when. Allow others to plan around you and understand your world. And that brings me to the most important person you need to communicate effectively with.

Yourself. You need to be able to realistically predict your own reactions to things. To understand when something going on inside you is going to make a book take longer, or make some element of the process harder for you to let go of.

Some stories matter to me more. Some stories have more of my journey in them. I was writing one recently where I'd included a traumatic event that I myself have experienced. I didn't write it any slower. If anything, I needed to write it faster, but oh my gosh was I very emotionally fragile during it. I ate so much chocolate. And I wasn't fun to live with. I should have known that I wouldn't cope as well during those few days. I should have had that internal conversation and understood my own needs.

It can also then spill out into other aspects of our work. I know I'm going to need my editor to be more gentle with some of those scenes. To understand they're more personal than normal. Good communication means owning up to this sort of thing and letting the people around you know what matters and what doesn't as much.

I also recently went through this with my cover designer. I use the same one for most of my self-pubbed books, and I've got one series that means the world to me, my epic fantasy Winter series. I have a very clear idea of what the main character looks like in my head, and very definitely what she isn't. When I first got mock-ups back from my designer, it was clear I hadn't communicated clearly enough what I was looking for.

So I spent two hours finding the right sort of images on stock sites and all sorts of other places. In the end I couldn't find what I wanted, but I could find enough different body parts, items of clothing and heads with the right elements that my designer could literally merge it all together to get what I wanted. It was important to me, so it was down to me to make sure my cover designer realised what mattered and what didn't.

And this also touches a little on support, which I'll elaborate on in a moment. Understanding your internal dialogue and communicating that effectively with others makes it far easier for them to support you in the way you need.

And on that note, let's move on to the next chapter.

Accountability and Support

Being a writer, or any other form of creative, is often a very lonely career path. Most creatives and writers sit alone all day, tapping out words. And it can make it hard to carry on, be motivated, and not, over time, become a little mentally unstable.

Not only is it important to have people to talk to for our own sanity, but having people around us who understand our dreams, goals, motivations and the importance of all that is huge.

I feel I need to add a caveat here. There are people you shouldn't tell your dreams and goals to. You need these people to believe the best in you, to cheer you on, and on occasion to give you a kick up the butt to get on with it. Sadly, there are a lot of people out there who respond to big dreams and goals in a negative fashion. Partially because they heard the same words from someone else and they don't realise they are simply replicating negative behaviour, and sometimes because they've hit a hurdle in their own dreams and goals and have given up, so they have lost hope for others succeeding.

While this can do you a lot of damage if you're hyped up about a brand-new dream or goal, if you find yourself in this situation, try to disengage, even if that means literally walking away from someone and then calming down. It will hurt, and you shouldn't feel ashamed of that, but once you've put some distance between you and them, you can think about why they reacted the way they did, and the truth is probably very sad.

The truth is, they're not you, and not everyone dares to dream big. And they've either let their dreams be crushed out of them by life or others. You don't want to be them, and you never know, if you keep pushing you might one day inspire these same people to try again. But it's important you don't rely on them either. Instead, you need to find a group of people, or, to begin with, even just one person, who can be your accountability and support in some way.

Sometimes just the act of telling people you're trying to do something can be enough. NaNoWriMo encourage writers to share on social media. As do the Inktober folks. Sharing goals like this can be a great way. But again, zap negative comments that pull your dreams down. You don't need negativity at this stage.

There are other ways you can make yourself accountable, but in general having relationships and good communication works best. This also then allows you the ability to form a support network of some kind or to join one.

Over the years I've been a member of many different groups. I've run a writers' group for a while, and I've joined Facebook groups and Discord channels (servers a person hosts on the Discord platform). It takes time to find and build a support group, but just like with accountability, you can start with just one person.

One of my early accountability and support buddies was my grandma. I gave her a copy of my very first book, and a couple of months later, out of the blue, she phoned me up and told me how amazing she thought I was. She didn't know it, but at the time, I was struggling to plot out the next book. Her effort to phone me up just to tell me she thought it was amazing how these ideas just came to me gave me the boost I needed to knuckle down and plot the next one. I still remember that and the calls after the next three books to this day, and it's been almost nine years since that very first one. I always gave her print copies after that. Always.

My grandma isn't alive anymore, as I've also mentioned, but these days I've got others who I talk to when I'm struggling. I've got my own Discord channel, with a mix of other writers, beta readers and general fans, along with a few close friends. No matter what is going on, they're there, full of encouragement, excitement and kind words. Even some advice occasionally. And I make sure I'm there for them in return. I want them to feel supported too. Because if encouragement and genuine excitement for each other's achievements is reciprocal, it only fuels more of it.

A very wise person once said that a rising tide lifts

all boats. And they're right. A group of people all striving and achieving and genuinely happy for each other also give the rest of the group inspiration and motivation to achieve. You show each other what's possible.

So, if I encourage you to do nothing else, I would encourage you to find some of these people. People who are genuine about their support of others. And then go support them in return. It can't be all about you and what you need. If you want genuine connection and people to support your creativity, you have to reciprocate. There will be seasons when you'll need more support or they will. And sometimes one of you will be having a bad day, but you'll get as much out of helping support them as they will out of supporting you, providing you're all striving towards goals and getting there eventually.

You can find a group like this in many ways. You might already have some among your family and friends, but if not, there are almost always groups set up. Most towns and cities have a writers' group of some kind. While not all of these will be the right fit, they're worth checking out. Even if they're not perfect, you might find one or two similarly minded people and be able to message each other when the group isn't meeting.

Or social media can often provide these groups and connections too. I've met and continued to converse with many writers this way. Some of my earliest support has come from one group in particular. I even found my editor and cover designer through them. And they've pushed me to take my career far more seriously than most would have done. In return, I do what I can for them when I can. I tell them what worked for me, and I share their work with my fans too, and when they're having a difficult time I see if I can help.

In no time, you'll find yourself surrounded by people like these. And it will make it easier to reach those goals, until one after another you find yourself climbing higher than before.

Summary:

- Find other positive people who believe in you.
- Tell them what you're up to.
- Both offer and ask for accountability and support in the right settings.
- Feed back. Check on them and offer what you can.
- Keep doing it.

Example:

- I've set up a Discord channel.
- I have sections for each of my books.
- I also have a sprint channel and general channel, where people can see the bits that apply to them.
- While I often vent on there, I also ask people how they are doing, encourage people to come chat when they're having bad days, ask if people want me to sprint with them, etc.
- I do this most days, and as frequently as needed.

WRITING

All of this brings us to the most important bit of all. The actual creation. In this section I'm going to talk about the writing itself. Because nothing is going to happen if we don't actually write.

In this section I'd also like to talk briefly about the different tools available to a writer. In this digital age there are a lot of great programs, apps and other stuff we can use to make our jobs even easier. Every writer is different, but we all need something to write with and some way of keeping it organised. And backed up.

I'm going to talk a bit about the different techniques to writing often and well, things like routine, teaching the brain to know what's going on, habit forming, and exercising the brain just like any other muscle. Habits are wonderful, and routine is something the human brain naturally loves. Although a lot of creatives love spontaneous things as well, routine does a lot for making creativity easier. Rituals can trigger brain systems and wake up our brain in the right way too, so I'll be talking briefly about those.

Finally, in this section I'd like to talk about methods of writing quicker. The effect sprints, practice and all that sort of thing can have. Humans don't naturally concentrate for long periods of time well. Creatives even less so. Sprinting can make a huge difference to productivity. And in certain settings it can even help beat procrastination.

All of this section focuses on one thing I've already touched on: how writing is a lot like training a muscle. You want to get truly good at something, you've got to train at it. This section focuses on the physical elements of that training. We've done the why you might want to train this muscle, and we've talked about the mentality and headspace you need not to give up. Now this is the nuts and bolts of actually doing it.

TOOLS

This is probably going to be one of the driest sections of this book, because I'm going to be talking about tools, but I'd seriously urge you to consider this section carefully, even if you already have a writing setup you love. More than once in my career as a writer I've made a tweak in an area listed below and seen a step up in productivity from it. If I'd stuck with the old faithful, I might still only be writing 500 words per hour and hating a massive swathe of the process to get a book from my head into the final manuscript.

Writing programs:
These are the tools we use to write. The very most basic one of these isn't a program at all. It's pen and paper. While this is almost definitely the slowest, it's also one of the best for dragging the brain, when it's kicking and screaming in protest, into writing mode. I started off writing by hand. It helped me

think better and the words flowed more easily. And in a lot of ways I still do. I still plot by hand, and fill in a paper ideas journal on a regular basis. Although long-term, for much higher word counts per hour, I recommend going beyond this option, don't be put off coming back here, or using it for the part of the process that needs it most.

Equally, there are a lot of different types of writing programs out there now. I won't list them here, but chances are your computer or laptop, and even tablet, will come with some these days. I use no less than three different ones on a regular basis. And sometimes, when I've done work for other people, I've used a fourth for a short while. This is definitely something you should experiment with.

I often use Google Docs on my phone. It syncs naturally with my computer, and then I paste this into LibreOffice at the end of the day. When on my laptop, I write in neither of those, preferring a much more basic system that's tied into my motivation. I'll come back to that later, in Motivational Programs.

One of the writers I work alongside most swears by a program that allows him to enter characters, scenes, places and all sorts of other details and create notes based on these, then tie them together visually —Scrivener. Every time he loads up the program, he can pick any scene note anywhere in the story and get writing.

For fantasy writers, I think this is a phenomenal way to approach it. There's a lot more to keep track of when you're inventing an entire world, universe, civilisations, religions, monetary systems and everything that goes with it. Having it all at your fingertips is great. There are a lot of other writing programs out there that allow this level of customisation and the ability to show it to you in different ways. Most also have free trials. If you need a free option, Wavemaker and SmartEdit do a reasonable amount too, and have been recommended by friends. And like all the tools, you can get recommendations in a lot of different writers' groups and hangouts.

Yet other friends like using notebooks or journals. Experiment, work out what you need and how you need it. Try other methods now and then.

Which also brings me to dictation. If you want to truly up your words per hour, this can be a wonderful step forward, but it does require some practice. It also requires some space to yourself, or somewhere you can go. If you like taking long walks, this can be perfect. You can walk, talk out your story, and then come home and edit. Whenever I hear people talk about this, they've recommended Dragon, but it's also possible to do some basic stuff on your phone with voice recognition, etc.

Personally, I write so cleanly as I go fast that I find the error correction time removes the bonus writing speed, and I would rather spend less time editing and a little more time writing. But I won't discount this forever. As technology gets even better at voice recognition, and as I get better at speaking—I'm starting to podcast to aid with this—I expect I'll make this switch at some point.

Backup programs:
I can't say this one enough. Losing writing hurts so

frelling much. Don't lose yours ever. Back it up. There are at least two popular backup services. Dropbox, that syncs with all your computers automatically as long as you save files within it, and Google Drive, that just needs a web browser. I use both for my raw writing and just one for my finished files. Google Drive, I use mostly because it also acts as a writing platform and syncs to my phone and tablet as well as my laptop, but Dropbox because it allows me to share files with others more easily and can handle a wider variety of file types and organisation systems.

Whatever useful extra features you want, make sure your work is backed up. Always. Don't log off without knowing your work is saved in the cloud somewhere. Or if you really don't trust it, then use something like Boxcryptor, or at the very least an external hard drive. Please.

Motivational programs:

This is probably one of my favourite most recent finds. I am going to thoroughly recommend the one I use most here, although I've refrained from doing that elsewhere, because this made such a huge difference to my writing I honestly can't sing its praises highly enough.

I love 4thewords.

It requires an internet browser and isn't great on the phone yet, but oh my frelling Enkoloth, did it make me write faster. Let me go into more detail about what it is and what it does for me. In essence, it gamifies writing. It makes the very act of writing a way of playing a game. On the website there are quests, monsters to fight and items to collect. Each monster has a set number of words you have to write if you want to defeat it, and a time limit. If you write those words within that time, you beat your monster. And if you don't, you lose. Collecting items from monsters that have been defeated and from missions you've completed allows you to progress in the game, get stronger and beat even more monsters.

On top of this, the website keeps track of a bunch of really useful stats, from things like the amount of days in a row you've written 444 words or more (this is how I know I'll get to 1000 days on May 4th), how many words you've written each day, month, year, etc., and how long you've spent doing it.

This has many different aspects that act as motivators for me. Who wants to break a long writing streak? Especially when there are rewards for getting those words written too. And who wants to lose to a monster? I found that playing the game for even a few weeks upped my sticking power. If you've got a monster that needs 2k words to beat it, you're going to stick your butt in your chair and write 2k words. I get distracted a lot less now. And 4thewords is to thank for creating my habit.

Of course, it's not the only motivational program— it's just the one that really hit the spot for me. I've got friends who use more extreme ones that lock down their computers until they've written X amount of words, or ones that even start deleting words if you stop writing for too long.

And there are some very basic ones that merely keep track of your streak, or overall stats, allowing the numbers themselves to act as motivators.

What you need and what works for you will vary, so just like anything else, I urge you to experiment and try all sorts. It might take a little perseverance to get used to something new, but you can get there.

Editing programs:

While I personally think nothing is better than a good editor, sometimes that's not an option, and a piece of work needs editing. A few writing programs have the basics built in, spelling and grammar checks, and I use these as far as they're helpful, but there are also a few websites that allow you to paste your words in or upload files and they give you some basic feedback on certain types of errors, things you might want to change and stuff like that. You may find that as you write more and get better you won't need one of these forever, but they can be great at the beginning. They help you learn some of the basic rules of writing, help clean up a manuscript so an editor later will have less work to do, and they are definitely better than nothing. Grammarly is one that's meant to be good. Research could turn up others.

Collaboration options:

There are also some tools for this. Some programs allow you to share files and both work on them simultaneously. Anything that aids collaboration is wonderful. Of course, it depends on how you collaborate, but there are tools that make this easier than others. Google Drive is probably the easiest, free way if you have more than one person working on a document. They've set themselves up to handle this well. And they back it up for you too.

Instant feedback tools/programs:

There are some great websites that allow you to put up chapters of your work and get feedback from a group of peers. They can be a great way to test the waters with early stages of work, or when you're newer as a writer. While few lead to monetary rewards, they're a way to see if an idea is working. I still use Wattpad now for a penname I launched recently. Wattpad is a social site built around being able to publish a story chapter by chapter and have people read and like/vote for these chapters. They have community-run competitions and awards, and all sorts of other interesting things going on. Sites like this can provide support and community too if you find the right set of people.

There are also a few of these run by publishers with an algorithm that eventually leads to work being seen by an editor from the publishing house. They can require a lot of work, but if your end goal is traditional publishing, they're a possible route.

My only caveat to using these sorts of sites is that, as I mentioned in the accountability and support chapters, you sometimes need to understand where others and their well-meant advice are coming from. Not everyone's advice should be listened to, nor everyone's criticism. You need to be honest with yourself. Don't change something that matters to you just because someone told you to. And protect your writer voice once you've discovered and honed it. If we all followed the writing rules all the time, we'd all write exactly like each other.

Publishing programs:

Finally, there are an awful lot of publishing-related programs out there as well, especially useful for those going the indie route. Programs that make formatting for print and eBook easier and things like that. If you know what you're doing with the more standard writing software, you don't always need this, but the last thing you want when you've worked hours and hours over a book is to feel like you're falling at the last hurdle to seeing it published, especially if you're money-poor and have a strong desire to go the indie route. Draft2Digital is probably the best here for eBook, and Vellum for print (Vellum does cost, but it's a one off).

Personally, I can whip a manuscript into shape with a normal program, but it's a steep learning curve for some.

I've not gone into actual ways to publish here, although there are many tools and platforms for this as well. I'm considering the publishing practicalities outside the remit of this book, but there's more than one platform for that too currently. And more than one type.

So I'll just leave you all with the same caveat I've attached to most of this. What works for you is probably personal. We're all unique individuals with unique motivations, goals and dreams. If you do nothing else with this section, let it inspire you to look for the best way for you. And never be closed to changing that in a few years' time, especially when life might have changed your priorities.

ROUTINE AND HABIT

Habits are a wonderful thing if they're good for you. There are a lot of good quotes about them too. But my personal take is that they should be something we take control of. We should strive to form good ones, and break bad ones, because life is easier once we have. Habits form a strong marker on our brains, and if something is done often enough we can even change our brain's entire makeup.

Writing regularly, or creating and seeing that we are being successful, ought, in my opinion, to be a habit. Habits are what build a muscle and keep it strong.

I was told a story about a pianist when I was younger. He practised every single day for half an hour, no less, and often more. And when asked why he did this every day, he replied, "When I have a day off entirely, the next day I can notice it a little. It is a teensy bit harder. If I take two days off, I really notice it and have to spend at least half an hour getting back into my usual state."

It can be tempting not to write at all, especially when you're doing other tasks, but I'd highly recommend doing a little every single day. My base line is 500 words, but to be honest, barely a day goes by that I don't do at least 1000 now. And it's now so much of a habit, if it gets towards the end of the day and I've not written, I feel wrong. Like I've been holding my breath just a little too long and can't quite get comfortable. And the only way to fix it? Write at least 500 words.

Habits are also something others respect. Not always because they approve of a habit, but others are as comforted by seeing people do something normal for them as we are by doing it. If you sit down and write every day, people will get used to you sitting down and writing every day. And they'll even begin to subconsciously make time for it. It becomes familiar for everyone.

And on that subject, John Cleese has spoken many times on the subject of creativity. Not only does he recommend that you create regularly, but he recommends that you do it at the same time of day. That way it becomes part of the daily ritual of life, not just something you squeeze in at the end before you crash. Now, there are definitely seasons were the end of the day before you fall asleep at the laptop is all you can offer your creativity, and you shouldn't beat yourself up about that, but if you can, doing it when you're a bit more at your best can do wonders.

The great thing is your best time of day will also be something you can discover by experimenting. It isn't the same for everyone. For some people it's firmly in the middle of the night, for others early in the morning. Again, if you can't experiment because you've only got the time you've got, then don't lament it too much. I know I write best between midnight and two a.m., but I have small children who wake me up around seven every morning. Sleeping for only five hours a night is just not enough for me.

Instead, I write in the evenings mostly, and whenever else I get a chance and need to. You should work out when you can create most consistently and stick to it.

As always, there are a few caveats. Sometimes another aspect of your life has to come first. Health, emotions and unforeseen circumstances all play a part. It shouldn't break your schedule if the worst did happen and you truly couldn't write or work one day, even two or three. You have to take care of yourself too, and I talk a bit more of that in another chapter later.

Another technique I love and use to help my brain switch into writer-mode quickly, something really useful when you've got other demands and a very little window to write, is to have a small pre-writing ritual. Many writers over the years have talked about their habits and pre-writing rituals and how they find it easier to get into the writing zone when they have a clear set of small tasks that lead into it.

I've also found one of these is pretty effective.

For me, I turn on the laptop, arrange my notebooks and pens down one arm of the chair I'm sitting on, or if I'm in a café down one side of the table. Then I will get myself a drink. If I'm at home, this means often filling my water bottle, and if I'm out, it's making sure I've got something cold and fresh that won't go bad if it takes me a while to get to it.

Then I open up my Discord server and see if other writers are around to write with (more about that in the next chapter), and while I'm waiting for other writers, I'll log into 4thewords, pick some monsters to fight and quests to chip away at and open up my WIP. Once my WIP is open, I'll have a read of the last page or so, not letting myself get too critical about what it says. I might fix an odd typo, but I don't want to wake the critical side of my brain —rather the creative one. Then I'll grab pen and paper and jot a few notes of what I want to write in the next 1-2k words. If I'm planning a bigger writing session, I might put down notes for more, but I've found only 1-2k ahead does best.

At this point I'm sure some of you will be saying, "But I've already plotted the book," and a whole bunch of you will be saying, "But I don't plot. I'm a pantser." In both cases, I seriously recommend doing it anyway. It's not something you have to follow if you're a pantser, and if you're a plotter, it's not meant to replace your previous plotting. What it does is begin to get the brain in the right gear, and it also serves to freshen your mind on what you were working on last time. It's one of my favourite techniques if I'm struggling later on as well. Just pick up a pen and a piece of paper and jot a few notes on the next scene or two.

After a little bit of plotting, and reminding myself of the characters and what's going on, I'll schedule up a sprint, set my monsters off, and write my little socks off.

Although it seems like that's a massive ritual and it would be hard to do that and still get some writing done, in reality it takes no more than about five minutes, and now I'm used to it, it feels really natural. It can also be a good reset, if interrupted, to repeat elements of it.

Of course, there are always times when doing the whole routine isn't possible. I tend to find I don't always need to do elements of it, but I try to do as much as possible of it and all of it at least once every other day.

I don't intend to tell you how to write as such. I think most creatives usually know their own process at least a little by the time they've finished their first major project, but I do know that the brain can be trained to want to create, and habits and rituals trigger its natural responses. Given enough time and enough repetition, you can train yourself to want to create on cue.

After I've written, I like to spend a few minutes winding down, thinking about what will come next. I also always stop in the middle of a scene, sometimes even in the middle of a sentence. This doesn't work for everyone. I know others who hate doing this. They completely forget what they were trying to say and have to delete what they had at the end. Figure out which works best for you and do that.

Finally, I like to record what I've done in terms of words and update my logs. I try not to do more than that most days, but about once a week I might take stock, update my goals for the next few weeks. If I'm having a good patch, I might up my goals for a few days to harness the best of that, or if I'm close to a deadline or the end of a book, I might aim a little higher. The purpose is to try and make the best of whatever is coming out and how well it's going.

Summary:

- Work out when during the day is best to write.
- Form a habit around this time.
- Defend it from others until they find it normal to allow you to do it.
- Create a short 5-10 minute pre-writing ritual.
- Write.
- Log counts and time.
- Feel satisfied with your achievement.

Example:

- I write in the evenings although midnight to two a.m. would be ideal. I try to start by eight p.m. and be done by ten p.m. Ideally, in the future, I'll also take a walk beforehand.
- I try not to arrange anything else during this time, with a couple of exceptions. If I can't write, then I try to write just before or after.
- Ask people not to disturb you. Don't answer calls. Talk about your writing if people disturb you.
- I like to be comfy, have a drink and my notes to hand. I just get them all ready in the same order each time.
- Words, and more words, and monster

slaying, mission-completing goodness.

- Open up spreadsheet, add in new words, assess on Sunday evenings. Re-plan the next week if necessary.

- Look to the next task or the next element, and if all that's done, relax or finally get some sleep.

PRACTICE AND SPRINTS

Now this is kind of an extension from the previous chapter. Habits are a way of practicing regularly, but I think there's a little more to practice than just forming a habit. When we practice stuff we're deliberately trying to get better at it. I'm going to assume that you're already dedicated to learning the craft of writing, or whatever you create.

This chapter is more about practicing the act of writing itself. Practicing getting into the zone, practicing forcing the muse to turn up rather than waiting for it, practicing discipline by making yourself do the same thing at the same time each day, and practicing attitude and organisation.

But it's also about practicing concentration and output. Almost everything we do, the more we do it, the faster we get and the faster we can push ourselves to do it with little adverse effect. Practicing writing builds the writing muscle.

When I first started writing, I used to struggle to

write more than 300 words an hour. Two thousand a day was hard work and made my mind feel tired. NaNoWriMo was the biggest challenge I could ever comprehend. And I was often a mental mess by the end of it.

But day by day, by pushing myself a little harder, I grew far better at it. A few years later, I did a 60k NaNo and recovered after only a couple of days. And a few years after that I did an 82k NaNo and then still wrote 40k the following month. The year just gone I wrote 60k the month before NaNo, 108k during Nano, and 55k the month after, and I didn't even feel more tired than normal.

My typing speed has also gone up. I can type at 60wpm (words per minute) when I'm going at my top speed. I couldn't even come close to that five years ago. It's something that only changed with practice. There's no shortcut. You have to keep doing something to get better at it.

And that brings me to one of the other big things that made a difference for me. Sprinting. The concept is also known as the pomodoro technique. The idea being that you set a timer, traditionally for 15-25 minutes (whatever works best for you), and then you create, non-stop, not allowing yourself to do anything else. After that, you make a note of what you've achieved if it's measurable.

The theory behind this is that you're both training your brain to concentrate and teaching it use the part of it that creates without worrying about whether it's any good or not.

All creative people battle what's called imposter syndrome and the fear of failing. Sprinting, especially with or against others, helps bypass that fear and anxiety and get you creating sentences. Once they're down on the page, you can worry about whether they're any good. And often, the consistent approach and methods that keep you in the zone have a good impact on the flow of a story and things like character consistency. If your brain never completely leaves the universe you're creating and slips back into it easily, then you are less likely to forget important details.

The other great thing about sprinting is that it naturally breaks your day's goals down to a smaller chunk of time and a smaller amount of words. On days when I am aiming for a very large word count, I love sprinting. Not only does it help keep a hard day fun, but it also stops the large overall number from being quite so overwhelming. For a moment you can focus on just the goal for that sprint.

Which in turn helps to beat fear-based procrastination. One little sprint isn't that scary. But before you know it, you can have sprinted your way to several thousand more words than normal.

Another way sprinting helps is that it's natural practice. You're training your brain to focus on a task for a short space of time and not be distracted, especially if you're anything like me and want to write faster than those who are sprinting at the same time as you.

It also does a myriad of other things. It helps you not feel lonely. It can be part of a habit, and it can help you learn to type faster and more efficiently. If competitive sprinting is your thing, it can get you writing a very large word count in a short space of time as well. And it's yet another metric that over time you can use to give yourself a positive boost, when you realise you are increasing your average, or are able to push yourself to sprint and focus for longer.

So invite a few friends to join you, or get yourself one of those tomato timers and get yourself racing to an invisible finish line.

Summary:

- Practice makes perfect.
- Practice regularly.
- Push yourself to aim higher.
- Find people or a system or device to do sprints.
- Sprint to whatever length you deem best.
- Record the results.
- Do it again... but better.

Example:

- I decided to write every day for as much as I could bear.
- Most of the time I try to do better than I did before at something, but I know this takes time.
- I use my Discord server to schedule sprints.
- For ages, I've found 15 minutes effective, but I can do longer times if necessary.
- My Discord server keeps track of personal bests and a few other things.

- Sometimes I sprint as many as twenty times in one day.

WHERE'S THE MUSE GONE?

Sometimes, even when you put all the above together, it doesn't work. Sometimes you can have sorted your organisation, your emotions, have done your routine and you still can't seem to make any progress.

Very occasionally everything that normally works won't. This section has several chapters on what might cause the muse to plain refuse to play ball and why you might want to take a break, do something else, or actively switch things up a bit. If the previous section was focused on the physical element of the writing process, this one is on the reasons to rest and how to do so effectively.

First we'll look at burnout and exhaustion. These are words you're probably familiar with. You might not know the best way to combat them, though, or how to prevent them from creeping up on you. Most importantly, I'll talk about some methods to ensure you never reach burnout in the first place. Ways to keep yourself feeling fresh and ready for whatever the day brings. There's a lot of hard and, often, shitty tasks that go along with the full career. Some of these really hurt when in burnout or just completely exhausted.

In this section we'll also talk about the creative well, ways to fill it, ways to use different parts of it, and all the stuff that comes with our creative muscles. There can be more than one way to be exhausted, and more than one well or tank that needs filling. Your creative well is just one of them.

I also want to talk about using rewards and making sure you celebrate in this section. Although this ties in with being positive and finding ways to motivate yourself, I think it ties in with resting. There's not a lot better-feeling than finishing a book and sitting back with something yummy, a good drink, or a few good friends, and relaxing while basking in the satisfaction of having crossed a metaphorical finish line. Sometimes we get so busy we forget these small pleasures.

Finally, in this section I want to talk about expectations and being realistic. While this could have gone in the headspace section, this is more about the expectations we have of success, what success is, and being real with how much effort we've put in versus what we've got out of something. You need to be real with yourself. It's so easy to blame other things if things go wrong, and it's easy to attribute our successes to single events when we wouldn't have been in the right place to benefit from that event if it hadn't been for some hard work we put in earlier (perhaps even years earlier). You need to be honest with yourself.

And finally I've linked some spreadsheets and other resources in the back of the book that I thought you might find useful as companions to some of the things we've talked about.

BURNOUT AND EXHAUSTION

Burnout is one of those millennial words that seems to be thrown around by a lot of people these days. It's almost fashionable to have burnout in some spheres of influence and some circles of culture. Of course, burnout can be defined in a bunch of different ways, so that doesn't help.

For the sake of this book I'm going to define what I mean by burnout.

Burnout is a sort of combined emotionally numb state, where your emotions have sort of gone home and don't want to play, with a complete lack of motivation borne out of exhaustion. And to elaborate a bit more, it's when you can't find the motivation for even bigger exciting tasks because they don't hold any emotional value for you now that your emotions are switched off. It makes it almost impossible to do the smaller, lower-reward but higher-effort tasks, and difficult to do the things you'd normally love doing.

A sort of exhaustion so extreme even your emotions are too tired to help you out.

I think this comes about in two ways. Firstly, when we stay in an exhausted state for too long, a lack of hope drains the rest of our emotions and capacity away with it. This is either do to with doing too much, or with being too inefficient about our recharge time. Or, secondly, we don't process our emotions well enough, or harness them properly. This allows us to get tugged around by them until we're so emotionally spent we're numb and trying to compensate with other stuff.

Tackling both burnout and exhaustion requires both self-awareness and self-care. It's no good thinking you're just exhausted when you're in burnout, and it's no good taking a physical rest and watching a movie when what you need to do is process some pent-up emotion of some kind. Life doesn't always make this easy, but sometimes you need to say no to a few things, push your schedule back, and just relax, give yourself space to think, and to not be frightened of your emotions.

If it's just exhaustion, then taking a break is clearly the best remedy. Sleep, some decent food, a drink and putting your feet up for a day or so can be enough to right your world again. Then remembering to do so on a regular basis as well, to try and keep yourself from getting so bad again.

Burnout is a different animal, however. If it's truly burnout, then it often takes a lifestyle change or a more permanent unburdening of a load to recover. It's rarely solved with a single day, but something that you recover from over time. Your emotions need time to start working again, and your desire to think about your goals and dreams needs to return.

During this state it's possible to get creative things done, but it's definitely not wise to push yourself as you were doing before it happened. Given how restorative creating for enjoyment can be, I'd recommend putting a small something on the goals list that you find very enjoyable. Something that doesn't have a deadline or any other purpose other than it's something you'd like to create. It doesn't even have to be the same type of creativity.

Of course, stopping burnout and exhaustion before they happen at all is going to be the best way forward.

The most important element is to identify their onset early. Are you already finding it hard to be motivated? Are you already struggling with certain tasks beyond the usual levels of imposter syndrome and procrastination?

If so, schedule in something fun that makes you feel better, some recharge time. And be strategic about when and how. We've already talked about communication with yourself and knowing what's going on with your emotions. It's a great idea to think about what helps you recover emotionally.

Personally, I'm an extrovert. I love being around people. So writing and working hard for a long period of time by myself is incredibly draining. I need regular things in my week to make me feel better and give my emotions a boost. To feel good feelings and to relax, especially on bad days, or when dealing with tougher elements.

I make sure my week includes everything I need it

to so I stay level. Very occasionally, in intense periods, some of these things get pushed out. If I'm close to a deadline. If one of the kids is sick, but most weeks these things, which are crucial to my wellbeing, are protected. I'll talk more about the exact things, what makes a good recharge activity, and all that sort of stuff in the next chapter, as this one is a lot more about the how, not the what, of burnout and exhaustion.

Some of this comes back to goal-setting as well. You might find that you're overdoing it. If so, consider adjusting your goals by 10%, aiming for a lower wordcount or a longer period of time to spread it over.

This whole process is like a lot of the others. You need to experiment, work out what you need, what only 'sort of' matters, and what just has to be done. But it's also important that you challenge yourself a little. A small patch of exhaustion in your life won't do you any long-term harm. As long as it's short enough.

Some of the happiest times of my life have been when my life was so full that I was exhausted at the end of the day from spending time with my children, working and living. If your working is helping you reach your goals and you have some meaningful relationships, being exhausted each day can feel totally worth it. And although I don't know this for sure, I assume that being exhausted because you're living a happy life to the full doesn't lead to burnout in quite the same way.

As before, you need to be honest with yourself, exercise self-care, and find the balance you need, even if you find it easier to switch between extremes instead of pacing yourself.

Summary:

- Burnout is far worse than exhaustion.
- Identify both and be honest with yourself if you're suffering from either.
- Take them both seriously and give yourself time to recuperate.
- Try to stop both from happening with a sensible lifestyle.
- Work out what is most effective in helping you recharge.
- Do it often enough.
- Feel better and find creativity easier.

Example:

- I came very close to burnout towards the end of October 2019.
- I was in denial for a couple of months, until I realised I was pushing too hard and it was costing me.
- Over the course of the next few weeks, I added some socialising back into my life. I'd been working non-stop to get my 2020 books ready, going to bed late, woken by the kids early.
- I knew it had to end. I planned some one-off activities until I knew things would get a little easier, and then more permanent ones after that.

- Some of my new activities were weekly, some only monthly, but it's a good start. I am still experimenting with what works best while having small children.

- Since I started taking better care of myself, I've upped my production per hour by about 10%. I'm better rested and therefore working better.

RECHARGING: BOREDOM AND CREATIVITY WELLS

I've talked about needing to recharge in the previous chapter and various other places. There are two big reasons we need to recharge. I've touched on one—burnout and exhaustion. The other is to refill our creative wells. Obviously not all the recharge methods work for both, but some do. The needs of both should be held in mind, weighed up, and then balanced against progress towards those goals and dreams you've decided on.

We need to recharge our creative wells, not grow bored and challenge our minds.

For those who have plenty of time, this can be done by watching TV or movies, reading books, playing games, going for walks, socialising and all sorts of other things. However, all those require quite a time commitment to be effective. And I'm a time-poor mother of tiny humans.

Therefore I've developed a slightly controversial technique of genre-hopping. As I've already said, I write in three genres under two names. It's considered a controversial strategy because not all fans read all genres, and some authors worry that they'll lose readers faster than they gain them because they're writing something else.

And it holds true, to some degree. People don't like to wait too long for sequels. With a long-enough gap, some readers will just go and find someone else's books to read. These are all good reasons for writing in one genre. Also, mastering one genre's craft is quicker and easier than mastering three genres' craft. And the genres can be very different. The tropes are different. The writing styles can even be different.

But these naysayers don't take into account boredom, and the need to recharge, nor does sticking to one genre allow for as much room to grow. And finally, it doesn't speak to the hundreds of pulp fiction writers with many pennames, publishers and books out each year.

When I tried to stick to the advice of writing one genre and one series at a time, I quickly grew bored around the beginning of book three, and sometimes every book thereafter. I couldn't keep myself writing no matter how hard I tried. And the point of this book is getting it all done. I can't claim to get it all done if I'm always stuck on book three.

Recently, almost by accident, I began to work out what books I had and which ones were ready to go. I noticed I'd started quite a few, so with very little effort I finished them. But I finished them because they weren't the usual books. I'd given myself free rein to jump between them and write whatever was flowing well.

Most of my books then got done far quicker than I expected. Every time I felt dry in one genre, I switched to another and felt like a new person again. Now I plan for exactly this. One book every 12 weeks in a genre, and three genres. Happy fans and happy me.

As soon as I implemented this strategy my average word count soared from about 800-900 words per day to over 1600. A doubling in effectiveness, pretty much.

The fans of the single genre know they're still getting a book every 12 weeks, and so does everyone else. But I have the other genres staggered in between, allowing anyone who wants to the opportunity to read everything in them all.

As far as I'm concerned, this made three genres the best way to operate (for me). I write the main series as I normally would in terms of speed, but I'm publishing almost three times as much. And I'm enjoying it more too. I also started to utilise soft deadlines and hard deadlines a lot here. Sometimes I need a longer break from a genre. I've not written much fantasy since finishing the fantasy epic for February's release. But I've done most of my penname books. The next fantasy book will still be done by the hard deadline, but I wrote something else instead for now.

When I'm further down the line and I've had some fantasy inspiration and enjoyment again, I'll be back on track for three genres. As long as I'm tracking the word count and making sure all the books are done by the hard deadline, then I won't have any long-term issues.

So, how else do I recharge? Surely I don't work all the time? Well, no, I don't work every minute of every day that I'm not sleeping or parenting. I do other things too. There are definitely some days when I'm so busy I do nothing else, but it can't be the norm. That way leads to burnout.

I've also mentioned before that I'm an extrovert. That means, for me, my recharge times often involve other people. But just like everything else in this book, I'm highly strategic about it.

On Monday nights I write with two friends. We talk plot, we talk life a bit around writing, and we sprint together. The sprints are fun, the plot conversations help me to not get stuck, and I feel supported as well as gain energy from the fun conversations.

Once a fortnight I meet up with some other writers as well. These are people I help more than I gain from, but they're still people to spend time with. We often sprint too, and talk about life, but the writing is secondary here.

Whenever I format, or do any job that is a bit more mundane and doesn't involve reading my own work, I listen to audio books. A recent study just proved this is akin to reading in terms of what it does to the brain. I get to relax, enjoy the formatting process a bit more than normal, and it helps me recharge those creative wells a little.

Once a week I take almost an entire day off. I say almost because, as I've said elsewhere, I always do a base minimum and I still have kids. I don't work in the evening though, and I always go to bed on time.

Finally, I regularly go to the cinema. Often on my day off. I love the cinema. The big screen and books are my favourite things in the whole world.

For the most part the combination of the above keeps me from going stir-crazy while still getting a lot done. You should identify what hobbies, activities and social activities help you feel calm quickest, recharge you emotionally, and also fill up that creative well, and plan them in accordingly. And then protect them. My day off never moves unless I can do it the day before or after instead.

Getting lots of stuff done also means taking care of yourself.

Summary:

- There are different things we need to recharge. Creative wells and normal emotional or physical capacities.
- You can recharge these in different ways.
- Balance each type of recharge and how you go about it.
- Work out what makes you feel better soonest.
- Do as much of it as you need to.
- Be honest with yourself about this too.
- Experiment. Rock your world.

Example:

- I have several recharge techniques, all of them used regularly.

- Moving genre to give elements of my creativity and desires a rest, I can keep all the fans happy and produce more books.

- I know reading and cinema are great for me, so I do both as often as I can.

- Then I take days off (or almost off) once a week.

- If I'm not feeling good, I ask myself if I need something else. Sometimes the answer is I need an hour playing games. Sometimes I need to finish a project and be pleased with myself for getting something hard done. If it's realistic to finish soon, I get something done.

- Things change, and I never hold my exact schedule too tightly. Only my hard deadlines are exactly that.

REWARDS AND CELEBRATIONS

If a lot of the other chapters have mentioned the stick, this one is very much about the carrot. This is where you give yourself something that's been dangling in front of you for a while.

Personally, I feel that the satisfaction of finishing something, especially a goal, is a pretty big carrot in and of itself. It's by far not the only one. But we'll start by talking about some of the less tangible carrots. Things like satisfaction. And then move on to the more physical sorts of rewards, instant gratification-style rewards, and all sorts of other things.

As I've mentioned already, satisfaction is part of the reward. When you've achieved something that's one of your goals, stop for a moment. Tell someone. The harder it was, the louder you should shout about it. I'm going to assume you have at least one person in your life who supports you and is genuinely excited when you achieve stuff. Tell them.

This is also a form of celebrating. Celebrate your successes, achievements, and especially if the goal is large, or you've reached a dream, have a party of sorts, or a dinner with the people who mattered in getting there.

I've thrown a party afternoon with a few friends. The first year I made three figures a month from royalties and had a series that was earning back its costs and getting into profit I invited my greatest friends over. They'd all been lovely and supportive. I used a month's royalties to get us all takeaway and drinks, and we played one of my favourite console games together.

I'm going to celebrate with a similar set of people on February 29th too. That's when my fantasy epic comes out. The book I've been working on since 2013 and first dreamed of in 2012. I don't know what I'll do yet, but just knowing I'll do something (and there will be physical books there), has kept me going through some of the toughest of slogs near the end.

There's also things like impact, and legacy. These mean different levels of things for different people, as well as calling/passions. If what you're doing is your calling or passion in life, it means more to you than anything else. That level of oneness with what you feel is your purpose and can be a powerful feeling and motivator. Are you doing what you feel like you were made to do? If so, remind yourself. Think about what that actually means.

Legacy and the impact we have on others can play a huge part in motivating us. Some of my friends used to print out their early fan mail and put it on their walls, especially if it made their readers' lives better in some way. Don't underestimate the importance of what you're doing in terms of what it can do for the world around you and what will be left behind when you're gone. Leave a legacy you're proud of.

The sole reason I decided to keep my penname books as opposed to three genres under my actual name, where all my releases could feed the one account, was because of my impact and legacy. The penname stuff helps more people. It brings more of a light into a dark place. And I get more fan mail from people whom I touched with my stories. That's so important. Don't let these things fall into the forgotten past. Save your fan mail. Print it out if need be. Write it in a journal just for this. Every time something you've created does something awesome, make a marker of some kind with it, so you can look back and be reminded when you need it.

I want to use an example of something not in a creative field here, because it's still one of the single best examples I can think of for both celebrating and putting a mile marker in the sand. There's a phenomenal anti-human-trafficking charity in the UK. Every single time they free a person and rescue them, they open a bottle of champagne. They celebrate. There were only a few in the first year, but every year after more have followed.

They then write that person's name on the cork. And they add it to a very special wall.

Over time they've built a wall, a wall of names and corks. After several people criticised this, saying things like, "Isn't it a waste of good charity money to open a bottle of champagne every single time?" they reconsidered what they were doing. But when they asked their staff, many of whom sat near it, walked past it, and saw it all the time what they thought, they all wanted to keep the tradition. Because on bad days it reminded them what they were capable of. When they were beginning to despair they would ever free a person again, or even just the person they were then fighting for, they looked at that wall and drew hope from it.

Find a way to build your wall. Be it testimonies, book titles, fan mail, a bookshelf, a wall of framed mementos. Anything that reminds you of the best bits, of the goals you've already achieved. On the really tough days, when writing yet another word feels like wading through the worst shit this side of a massive bat-invested cave, look at it. Remember how each of those successes felt. It will help you remember that fighting on a little longer is worth it. That you've done it before, and can probably do it again.

And this brings me nicely to the physical rewards. I love physical rewards for reaching milestones and goals. And I like them to be consistent, reliable, and at a sensible balance of frequency to be effectively motivating, but not so often that I get sick of that particular reward.

One of the things I found most amusing about the well-meaning parenting advice I've had in the last four years or so is to not give your children sticker charts, or reward-based pocket money. The reason being that apparently life doesn't give you physical rewards for doing the right thing, the chores, or behaving the way we ought to once we're adults, so we're training our children to need something that doesn't exist. This is hilarious, because, as an adult, I frequently reward myself for good behaviour, for doing the shit jobs, and for getting something right. Maybe I've not grown up, but if so, that works for me.

I do what I need to, I get chocolate. Because I'm as human as my children are, and what works for them works for me too.

But to explain a little better, and just in case you've forgotten, my rewards are once again tied into my goals or milestones, not dreams. The most basic one: every 15k words I write, I get a Crunchie chocolate bar. If you're not familiar with it, a Crunchie is a stick of honeycomb wrapped in milk chocolate. In this case, my favourite milk chocolate in the world. I always have a ten-pack of them in the fridge. No one else touches them. They're mine. Very occasionally I'll get one out and place it somewhere I can see while I'm writing. To taunt me over the finish line. The amount of days when I've written a few more hundred, and then a few more hundred words because it means I get a Crunchie is far larger than I expected it to be. It works.

But it's a potentially repetitive reward, and if I'm having a good writing patch, I can earn one of those every other day. I used to earn one every 10k, but I can write 14k in a single day at the moment if I push. I don't want to have it so frequently that I don't enjoy it anymore. Once a week holds this balance well for me. I'm aiming to write 2250 words a day on average, so 15k a week is a good number.

On top of that, every time I finish a book I have a drink. This varies, but it's often a fruit cider of some kind. I take a few minutes to kick back, relax, play a game or chat to a friend and have a drink. I don't always do it the second I finish a book. Sometimes it's a couple of days later, but I do it soon after, if I can. The only time I don't do this is if the story is under 30k. If it is, I'll do one every two stories. There's always a section of time each year when I write quite a few shorts and novellas. I don't need a drink every couple of days, etc.

The great thing is that you can make your own system in that regard. Whatever works for you. Do it often enough you feel like you get there, but not so often you find it loses its specialness too much.

There are also monetary rewards if that works for you. I've got several writer and author friends who buy themselves material things with their hard-earned career money either at particular milestones or with percentages of income. The material thing can be anything. With one friend, who ghost-writes, he literally works out how many £ he's earned that day from his writing (assuming he gets paid for it), and puts a percentage aside. When he has enough he buys himself a console game. Then he gets a day to play it before going back to the grind.

Find the motivator you need. Be realistic about if it's likely to happen and you'll get your reward. If not, back to the drawing board. Think of something else, try something else. Just don't forget about all the things you did that mattered.

Sharing exciting things like new cover designs and pictures of print books is always a wonderful way to generate the feeling of something new and exciting coming soon, as well. Use those along the way if you can.

Summary:

- There are two types of rewards. Decide which intangible ones mean something to you.

- Find ways to harness those more intangible rewards.

- Celebrate the bigger milestones, make a marker of the smaller ones.

- Decide if your legacy, impact and calling are important. Celebrate what is and make sure it doesn't stop with you.

- Change the world.

- Decide on some physical rewards.

- Tie them to goals and milestones.

- Reward yourself.

- Feel rewarded. Make use of unexpected reasons to get excited.

Example:

- Satisfaction of finishing works great for me. As does knowing I changed someone's life for the better.

- I keep fan mail, keep track of all the books I finished and remind myself of them. I also tell my fella lots of stuff. And my Discord server.

- I'm going to be having a party on December

4th, 2020. It will be ten years to the day since publishing my first story. And I'll be putting out my 20th in 2020 that day too.

- My calling is something I remind myself of regularly. I was born to tell stories in one format or another.
- Each books changes the world a little.
- Chocolate and fruit cider for the win.
- One every 15k, the other every book or two novellas and shorts.
- I've almost finished this book. Guess what is already chilling in the fridge?
- I also got a cover design today. I shared it on my Discord and used the thought of it coming soon to get through the edits.

EXPECTATIONS AND YOUR FUTURE

And this brings me to the end of the book. We've gone from taking our dreams, breaking them down into goals and a schedule, creating and sticking to deadlines, the discipline, initiative and organisation needed to stick to that, to the emotions we need to handle in order to beat procrastination and keep ourselves positive. We've talked about the importance of communication, both with yourself and with others. And honesty.

After that we talked about the importance of a good accountability group. One that genuinely believes in you and hopes for your success. Then the tools you need, both practically, but also with routines, rituals, practice and habits.

Finally we looked at burnout, how to recharge, and possibly most importantly of all, how to reward yourself, celebrate and mark the important and meaningful moments in what will also be your legacy.

But there's one more little thing I'd like to

mention before I go. It relates to all of them.

All through this book I've talked about things like being honest with yourself, using a carrot or a stick, difficult tasks and how to break them down. How to make life easier on your emotions. And many more things.

None of it will work if you're not realistic.

If you're going to set good goals and achieve your dreams, you need realistic expectations of what you're capable of and what you can achieve in a short space of time.

If you're going to manage your emotions through difficult times, you're going to need to have realistic expectations of your own emotional self-awareness and ability to process.

You also need realistic expectations of your support group. Even people who think you're awesome will drop the ball now and then. We're all only human. And the same goes for communication. You need to ask yourself a lot of questions and answer them honestly so that you can move forward knowing more about yourself and others.

You need to have realistic expectations of how long it takes to get something done. If you can write 700 words per hour, and want to write 35k a week, you need to spend 50 hours just writing. Not particularly realistic. However, if you can write 1.5k per hour and you're only aiming for 30k, then you'll only spend 20 hours a week writing—much more manageable. Unless you have another job, or kids, etc.

I'm also going to add a little something in here about not comparing yourself to others. Comparing yourself to other people blows realism out of the water. You become focused on what they're doing and how good it is until you're not happy with stuff you've done and achieved. You can only do the journey you are on, with the skillsets you have and the talents you have acquired.

Instead, I like to race myself, beat my own records. I use my own metrics of myself as a mile-marker. I love beating my personal bests. Many a time that's got me through NaNo. And it shows my progress too. It exercises my writing muscles and it keeps me striving towards the next goal.

So although you should be realistic, this doesn't mean you don't challenge yourself. Not one bit. You've got dreams to reach, and while your goals and expectations should be fairly realistic, your dreams should be as huge as you want them to be.

I have many dreams, some of them so much bigger than me. But I have realistic expectations of what I can control and what I can do. I'll dream anyway, and I'll keep trying, but I won't forget that little ripples I make in this life can spread far and wide. And the seemingly smallest moment can lead to the biggest breakthrough towards that dream.

I hope this book has helped you figure out what you can improve on. Ways you can work quicker. Ways to handle life around being creative. And that it's given you some tools to use in both the physical process of writing, but also the emotional process. Ways to beat procrastination, ways to motivate yourself, and ways to reward the end results.

In the journey of creating some form of artwork, it's never going to be all easy. Some days it's the toughest, smelliest crap. Some days it's so easy and feels so good it's effortless flying. Whatever kind of day it is, you need to start. And you need to keep trying. And you need to push yourself.

And there's one more thing I'd like to say. None of this book has any point or value to you if you give up for good. Day after day you need to sit yourself down and do something. I can give you loads of methods to make it easier, faster and less stressful, but you still have to make the decision day after day to keep going. I'll also make a bit of a confession here. I've failed many times. And I've given up. But only for the rest of the day. Each new day is a fresh start. Each new day your failures are behind you and you can try again.

So, how badly do you want this? How important is that dream? Really important? I hope so. Because only you can make it happen. But you're already on the way there. You're already changing the world, one moment, one goal and one milestone at a time. I hope you find the dream you're looking for, and that this book helps you on your journey towards it, even if only a little.

ABOUT THE AUTHOR

Jess was born in the quaint village of Woodbridge in the UK, has spent some of her childhood in the States and now resides near the beautiful Roman city of Bath. She lives with her husband, Phil, her two tiny humans (one boy and one girl) and her very dapsy cat, Pleaides.

During her still relatively short life Jess has displayed an innate curiosity for learning new things and has therefore studied many subjects, from maths and the sciences, to history and drama. Jess now works full time as a writer and mummy, incorporating many of the subjects she has an interest in within her plots and characters.

When she's not busy with work and keeping her tiny humans alive she can often be found with friends, playing with miniature characters, dice, and pieces of paper covered in funny stats and notes about fictional adventures her figures have been on.

You can find out more about the author and her upcoming projects by following her on her fanpage on facebook or emailing her via books@jessmountifield.co.uk. Jess loves hearing from a happy fan so please do get in touch!

LIST OF PRINTED WORKS

Fantasy:
Tales of Ethanar: An Anthology (Containing the first six Tales of Ethanar - Wandering to Belong, The Path Home, Learning to Fly, For Such a Time as This, A Fire's Sacrifice and The Hope of Winter) - Coming 2021
The Fire of Winter (Winter: 1)

Sci-Fi:
Sherdan's Prophecy (Sherdan: 1)
Sherdan's Legacy (Sherdan: 2)
Sherdan's Country (Sherdan: 3)
Adamanta
Excelsior

As Amelia Price:
The First Lessons: The first three stories in the Mycroft Holmes Adventures series (The Hundred Year Wait, The Unexpected Coincidence, and The Invisible Amateur)
The Second Chance: The fourth, fifth and sixth stories in the Mycroft Holmes Adventure series (The Female Charm, The Reluctant Knight and The Ambitious Orphan)
The Third Holmes: The seventh, eighth and ninth stories in the Mycroft Holmes Adventure series (The Unconventional Honeymoon Gift, The Family Reunion and The Immortal Problem)

With Dawn Chapman:
The Magic Sequence (Containing Jessica's Challenge, Dahlia's Shadow, and Lila's Revenge)

Non-fic:
How to Write Lots, and Get Sh*t Done: the Art of Not Being a Flake

Printed in Great Britain
by Amazon